A Professor's Guide to Writing Essays

The No-Nonsense Plan for Better Writing

Second Edition

Dr. Jacob Neumann

A Professor's Guide to Writing Essays (2nd Edition)
by Dr. Jacob Neumann

ISBN-10: 0-692-82252-6
ISBN-13: 978-0-692-82252-4

3203 Pelican Lake Ave.
Edinburg, TX 78539

Email me at: dr.jacobneumann@gmail.com

CONTENTS

HOW THIS BOOK WILL HELP YOU

I want to help you improve your writing. If you're a college student, a graduate student, or even a high school student, and you're serious about wanting to improve your writing, then this book is for you. I've been teaching since 1996. Now I work as an associate professor at The University of Texas Rio Grande Valley where I teach people how to teach. I've taught at every level of schooling, and I've taught students from around the world. So I know what students need to learn to do to write good essays. I'm also a scholar who publishes in some of the top journals in my field (you can look up my work on Google Scholar). So I know what it takes to write good essays in the real world of academic writing. In this book, I boil down all of my experience as a teacher and as a writer into a plan that will help you learn to become a better writer.

In this book, I'm not going to tell you any cute stories about writing. Instead, I get straight to the point, with a step-by-step plan, practical explanations, and examples that show you how this information works in published academic writing. I'm going to show you how to write an essay from the outside-in. This means that we're going to focus on the big picture and put our essay together in pieces. The purpose is to help you keep the big picture straight in your head. This will help the details make better sense. This method is different from what other books and teachers teach. But it works. I'm then going to show you some editing tips that will address some of the most common mistakes that students make when writing essays. At the end of the book, I include a long section on using citations, including specific examples of how to incorporate them into your writing just like a professor would.

In this updated second edition, I also give you a "quick guide" for writing an essay. This quick guide is an overview of the main points I show you in the book. It gives you a condensed version of these points so you can clearly see how the pieces of an essay are put together. This will give you an easy to follow model for putting your essays together.

STEP 1: MAKE AN OUTLINE

Most students don't make outlines of the points they want to write about. Instead, they just start writing. Maybe they think it's a waste of time or just not that useful. Whatever the reason, it's a mistake to not write an outline. Outlines do a lot for you. Outlines keep your ideas organized. They help you to not repeat yourself. They also help you to not contradict yourself. To make an effective outline, first list all of the points that you want to make in an essay. Don't worry about putting them into any order; just get them down on paper.

We're now going to start our sample essay, the one we're going to develop throughout the book. Our topic is "the difficulties in teaching Social Studies in elementary school." I teach in a College of Education, and this is a topic that I might assign to my students. We're not going to write a very long essay, but it'll be long enough to illustrate the steps. I first want to write down things I think I might want to write about. Don't worry about the order; we're just trying to get down some thoughts. Here are my ideas:

Standardized testing
Lack of time to teach
Lack of resources
Too much content – what to teach?
Does Social Studies even count?
Pressure to teach just facts
Schools focus on reading, math, etc

How do I know what I want to write about? Well, I'm drawing from my experience as a teacher, as a researcher, and as a professor. I've read a lot about the difficulties in teaching Social Studies in elementary classrooms. I taught elementary school a long time ago. I teach students who are thinking about becoming elementary teachers. And I know elementary teachers. So I'm going to draw on my knowledge from all of those sources to help me decide what to write about.

For your essay, you should carefully study the prompt that describes what you need to think about and write about. Then you'll probably have to do some research, some reading, and probably some more thinking. It doesn't matter what "type" of essay you're writing. You'll need a number of points to explain/discuss/argue in any of the essay types. Right now I just want you to write down some thoughts. They can be details or big picture ideas. At this point it doesn't matter; you just need to begin making a list of points you might want to make. Once you've made your list, then we can start to think about how we will order these points. Below, you'll see my initial thoughts and those thoughts revised into an order I think I might want to use:

Initial Thoughts:
      Standardized testing
      Lack of time to teach
      Lack of resources
      Too much content – what to teach?
      Does Social Studies even count?
      Pressure to teach just facts
      Schools focus on reading, math, etc

Revised Thoughts:
      Standardized testing
      Pressure to teach just facts
      Lack to time
      Schools focus on reading, etc
      Does it even count?
      Too much content – what to teach?
      Lack of resources

You might be asking how I knew to revise the order of my ideas. Well, my knowledge and experience tells me that standardized testing is usually a big factor that influences teaching. And several of these other factors act as a result of standardized testing (pressure to teach just facts, lack of time, schools' focus on reading, and does Social Studies even count). So, it makes sense to me to put it first. But if I was arguing different points, say only three points, then I might put the biggest point last to end on the strongest note. When you revise your initial thoughts into an outline, start by reviewing all of your notes and research on your topic. Then decide which order makes the most sense to discuss/explain/analyze the points you want to make. There isn't really any one best way to do it, regardless of what some teachers and books might tell you. It will vary depending on the essay you are writing and the points you are making. Instead of trying to find and follow the one "best" way, try to just decide what order might work best for the task in front of you.

With my revised thoughts, I now have an idea about body paragraphs for my essay. We'll study paragraphs in depth later, but for now remember that each idea gets its own paragraph. So my body paragraphs might look like this (remember that we'll also need an introduction and a conclusion, but we'll work on that later):

<u>Version 1</u>
Paragraph 1: Standardized testing
Paragraph 2: Pressure to teach just facts
Paragraph 3: Lack to time
Paragraph 4: Schools focus on reading, etc
Paragraph 5: Does it even count?
Paragraph 6: Too much content – what to teach?
Paragraph 7: Lack of resources

This paragraph order might work fine for my body paragraphs. But I can always change my mind if I think of a better way to organize my paragraphs. Maybe I want to do the following and reshuffle my ideas:

<u>Version 2</u>
Paragraph 1: Standardized testing
              Lack of time
Paragraph 2: Pressure to teach facts
Paragraph 3: Does it even count?
              Schools focus on reading, math, etc
Paragraph 4: Too much content
Paragraph 5: Lack of resources

The more I think about it, the more I might want to change my outline. At the least, this gives me two options for ordering the content of my essay. I'm still thinking about beginning with standardized testing. But now I'm thinking about including a lack of time in the paragraph about testing. Then I'm thinking about discussing the pressure to teach facts, because that is a common result of a lack of time to teach (teachers often feel that they must squeeze everything in). Then maybe I'll group together "does it even count?" with schools' focus on reading, math, etc. This is because the question about Social Studies counting is directly connected to their focus on reading and math. Then maybe I'll discuss the amount of content and the lack of resources, just like the first version.

Whatever your topic is, it's ok to give yourself some options as to how you want to organize your ideas. Assuming you've done good reading and research, you're in the best position to make that decision. Just remember that your outline doesn't have to be perfect the first time you put down your thoughts. It only improves after you put a lot of thought into it. You also don't need to know, at this point, exactly what you will write about within each paragraph. That will come as you begin to write them. Write the topic of your essay, write what points you might want to make in your essay, and then try to organize them into an outline.

STEP 2: WRITE A THESIS SENTENCE FOR YOUR ESSAY

After you've made your outline, and before you write anything else about your essay, I want you to write a thesis sentence for your essay. A thesis sentence is a sentence that explains what your purpose is for your essay. This sentence should guide your thinking about the rest of the essay. Don't worry if the language isn't exact; you can change that later. For now, you just need a sentence that you can use to focus your thoughts. Make this sentence simple and to the point. Don't use a lot of fancy words and definitely don't use any "fluff" (words that people think might sound good but don't actually mean anything). Let's create some possible thesis sentences for our sample essay. We're going to use the "Version 2" set of potential paragraphs.

> Paragraph Outline
> Paragraph 1: Standardized testing
>   Lack of time
> Paragraph 2: Pressure to teach facts
> Paragraph 3: Does it even count?
>   Schools focus on reading, math, etc
> Paragraph 4: Too much content
> Paragraph 5: Lack of resources

So, let's ask a basic question: what are all of these paragraphs about? Our topic is "the difficulty of teaching Social Studies," and all of these paragraph ideas focus on specific reasons why teaching Social Studies is hard. We need a simple way of saying that teaching Social Studies is hard for a lot of reasons. Here are three possible thesis sentences:

> 1. Social Studies is hard to teach for a number of reasons.
> 2. Teachers have a tough job teaching Social Studies.
> 3. A number of factors make Social Studies hard to teach.

Notice how simple these sentences are? To the point without frills or fluff. They are all pretty similar, and I can decide which one to use later. But they will focus my thoughts as I keep developing my essay. Some teachers, books, and guides will tell you that you need a "hook," some kind of "interesting" sentence to grab your readers' attention. This is a mistake. Don't try to be clever with your thesis sentence; instead, make your sentence functional. It should be broad enough to cover your topic, but specific enough to give me a sense of what the essay will be about. Nor do you need to cram everything into that sentence – that's what you'll do with the rest of your essay.

One last thought about thesis sentences. Say you have to write an essay that compares and contrasts Shakespeare's use of imagery in Hamlet and Macbeth. If you get stuck, try writing something like this: "This essay will compare and contrast Shakespeare's use of imagery in Hamlet and Macbeth." Now, you shouldn't actually use this as a thesis sentence. It doesn't sound that good. But it will get you going. Later, you can revise it to something like, "Shakespeare's use of imagery in Hamlet and in Macbeth has a number of similarities and differences." I will show you more examples of thesis sentences in Step 4. If you think it will help you to jump ahead and look at those other examples, please do. Now try to write some possible thesis sentences for your essay.

STEP 3: WRITE TOPIC SENTENCES FOR EACH PARAGRAPH

Now that you've made an outline and written a thesis sentence, I want you to write topic sentences for each paragraph in your essay. This probably sounds like a weird thing for me to ask at this point, and it might seem overwhelming. Most students are used to just writing an essay straight through. But remember how much trouble most students have with writing essays? That same old approach usually doesn't work that well. What we're doing here is different, but it will help you to develop your thoughts about the essay one step at a time. Here, I'm asking you to think about the topic of each of your paragraphs. It doesn't matter if your paper has 5 paragraphs or 25 paragraphs. You'll need to think about them eventually; you might as well do it now. We're developing our essay from the outside in. Also remember that these sentences don't need to be perfect. Nor do they need to be fancy. Just make them to the point. Also, you can always change them later. Right now you're just working on your ideas and structure for your essay.

Let's go back to the second set of potential paragraphs that we used in Step 2. Really think about each of those subtopics. What is each one about? What kinds of points might you make in each paragraph? Questions like these will help you to create sentences that are similar to the thesis sentence: broad, but focused enough to give the reader a sense of what the paragraph will be about. Below, I list each of the paragraph topics, I write a possible topic sentence for each of those paragraphs, and I give you a short explanation of why I wrote each of those topic sentences:

Body Paragraph 1
    Topic: Standardized testing, lack of time to teach

    Topic sentence: *Standardized testing shapes, and often limits, how Social Studies is taught.*

    Why: Since the topic of this paragraph is about how standardized testing can limit the time teachers have to teach Social Studies, as well as make it difficult to teach, I want to include both ideas in my topic sentence. The word "shapes" is key, because it creates a visual image of teaching being

8

molded and shaped by testing. Now, the rest of the paragraph will be about how standardized testing shapes and limits teachers' ability to teach Social Studies. Note that I don't technically need the commas around the phrase "and often limits." I use them because they emphasize that phrase.

Body Paragraph 2
Topic: Pressure to teach facts (related to standardized testing)

Topic sentence: *Standardized testing often creates an intense pressure to teach just facts.*

Why: The pressure to teach facts is linked to standardized testing. This subtopic deserves its own paragraph, but I need to make the connection to standardized testing. Note that "intense pressure" tells readers how strongly teachers can feel this pressure. I also use the word "often" because I can't claim that it always creates this pressure, just that it often can.

Body Paragraph 3
Topic: Does Social Studies even count? Schools focus on reading, math, etc.

Topic sentence: *The focus on tested subjects can de-emphasize Social Studies, since it often is not tested.*

Why: I don't need to specifically mention reading and math in this sentence. That'll come in the paragraph. It's enough to mention "tested subjects." By writing "de-emphasize Social Studies," I am referring to another difficulty, and making a connection to the fact that Social Studies is usually not tested. As I'm working on the paper, I might want to specify which focus, instead of just writing "The focus." Maybe I will change it to "Schools' focus." That would make it clearer about whose focus it is.

Body Paragraph 4
Topic: Too much content for teachers to teach

Topic sentence: *The sprawling nature of Social Studies content can also impact how it is taught.*

Why: I use the phrase "sprawling nature of Social Studies content" to give a visual of a lot of content to teach, so much that it "sprawls" across the classroom. The words "can also impact" work as a transition from paragraph 3 to paragraph 4. Notice that I again specifically mention how Social Studies is taught. I'll describe the effects in the paragraph.

Body Paragraph 5
   Topic: Lack of resources for teachers to use while teaching Social Studies

   Topic sentence: *Finally, a lack of resources can strain Social Studies teaching.*

   Why: This is probably the most basic of the topic sentences. I use the word "finally" as a transition indicating last of a list. I clearly state "a lack of resources" and that they can "strain" Social Studies teaching. Nice and simple.

Let's take a look at what we have so far for our sample essay. We have a potential thesis sentence for our introduction, plus potential topic sentences for 5 body paragraphs (for 6 paragraphs total, so far). I'll list them below:

   Introduction
      Thesis = Social Studies is hard to teach for a number of reasons.

   Body paragraph 1
      Topic sentence = Standardized testing shapes, and often limits, how Social Studies is taught.

   Body paragraph 2
      Topic sentence = Standardized testing often creates an intense pressure to teach just facts.

   Body paragraph 3
      Topic sentence = The focus on tested subjects can de-emphasize Social Studies, since it often is not tested.

   Body paragraph 4
      Topic sentence = The sprawling nature of Social Studies content can also impact how it is taught.

Body paragraph 5

        Topic sentence = Finally, a lack of resources can strain Social
        Studies teaching.

Now it's your turn. List the topics of each of your paragraphs and write topic sentences for them. Keep the sentences simple and direct, just like mine. Again, don't worry about getting it perfect; just get down the thoughts.

STEP 4: WRITE AN INTRODUCTION THAT WORKS

Effective introductions do three things: 1) they establish a context for your essay; 2) they clearly state what the essay is about; and 3) they (usually) give readers a sense of the points you'll be making in the essay. If your paper is relatively short (5 pages or less), you can do all of this in one paragraph. If your paper is longer, you might use multiple paragraphs for an introduction. However many paragraphs you use, you'll still want to accomplish the same things. Also, remember what I wrote about "hooks" in Step 2? The same directions apply here. Don't get distracted with a "hook." Great introductions accomplish these specific tasks; your writing will improve tremendously if you focus on these tasks.

Examples of Three Different Introductions

Let me make one crucial point here. Many teachers, courses, and books claim that students need to learn to write different types of essays: expository, persuasive, argumentative, etc. I disagree. Good writing doesn't change depending on a "type." All that changes is how you make your argument. It's important to bring this point up now, since introductions are where we can begin to see the similarities across different purposes (or "types") of writing.

I'll begin to illustrate this by showing you examples of introductions for different "types" of essays. We're not working on our sample essay right now. Right now I'm going to show you different ways of writing an introduction. We'll get back to our sample essay at the end of this step. Note that we're going to follow this pattern for the rest of the steps: first I'm going to discuss the information in the step and show different examples of how to use that information. Then, at the end of each step, I'm going to apply this information to our sample essay. Keep this format in mind and the rest of the book will be easy to follow.

The three examples that I show you below are taken from essays that I have published in academic journals, so you can be assured they are good quality. In these three examples, you'll notice that the writing is either bold, underlined, or italicized. These three markings show the different purposes of the text. Remember that introductions need to do three things, and usually in this order:

BOLD TEXT: sets up the context. It tells me a little bit about the background of the essay. You should use one or more sentences to express something that you've learned about your topic, from the research you've done, that will help readers to understand the context and purpose of your essay.

UNDERLINED TEXT: shows the thesis sentence. You've already written that, so all you'll probably need to do is to insert it here (unless you want to make any small changes in language so that it sounds as good as it can).

ITALICIZED TEXT: gives readers a sense of what points will be addressed in the essay. You don't want to give away all of the details, nor do you want to get too in-depth about any of your points. Save your analysis/argument for your body paragraphs. But you do want to give your readers some general ideas about what points you will discuss/examine/argue in your essay.

A "critical analysis" essay:

"Best practice" would seem to be the pinnacle of practice to generate learning inside the classroom. Borrowed from the language of business, it refers "to a set of techniques for most efficiently and effectively producing a desired outcome" (Lampert, 2010, p. 25), suggesting assurance for the educator, legislator, or parent wondering about what to do to improve learning in schools. It suggests that if we will simply implement *this* practice or *this* method, then education will improve. <u>However, important questions can also be raised about assertions of "best practice."</u> *First, while the language of "best practice" seems clear at first glance, its definition in the literature is not. Second, a range of teaching practices might reasonably be called serious, thoughtful, or responsible. But the word "best" implies a comparative hierarchy: not many practices, but select and specific practices. It is not clear, though, that this philosophy of teaching always best serves all contexts and* *purposes in schools. Third, and perhaps more importantly, for what goals and on what evidence is "best practice" based?*

In this example, notice how I get straight to the point. I first introduce what the idea of "best practice" means. I offer a definition from the literature, but I also use broad strokes. I don't want to get too detailed in the introduction. It almost reads like I am supportive of "best practices." But then I raise the problem with "However." We can call this point/counterpoint analysis. I make the point about "best practice," but then I turn that point around into a series of questions. The thesis sentence works as the "turn" in this case, in that the thesis sentence is used to turn around the analysis. After the thesis sentence, I list what the problems are with notions of "best practice." I examined these questions in the rest of this example essay.

A "persuasive" essay:

> **Social studies classes can often feel like a timed race over an obstacle course. In U.S. history classes particularly, the amount of information to be learned by students can present a significant challenge to both students and teachers. Not only is the breadth of information daunting, but helping students to make meaningful connections to what they often see as boring or irrelevant facts can make the task seem substantially harder. In addition, many students enter the class with little existing knowledge of U.S. history. <u>One simple tool for helping students make these necessary connections is called an "Act it Out."</u>** *An "Act it Out" is simply a short play in which students act out information (specific events or concepts) that they are learning in class. Incorporating drama into social studies classrooms is certainly not a new innovation. But when used as an occasional or even consistent tool to bring specific historical information to life, it can foster lasting benefits in students' learning. Using drama in this fashion helps students to not only visualize distant and complex events, making the abstract more concrete, but to gain a better understanding of the different points of view of the people involved, helping them to relate to these events at much deeper levels than through simply reading a text.*

Just like the first example, in this paragraph I begin by establishing the context. Then, in the thesis sentence (underlined), I offer a possible solution. After

I define what an "act it out" is, I offer some reasons why using "act it outs" can help improve students' learning. The writing is efficient: I want to create a context, but I only tell readers what I think they need to know. Just as important, I persuade readers to keep reading when I tell them some of the benefits of using "act it outs" in their classrooms.

A "descriptive" essay:

> **Teachers often struggle to integrate computer technology into their teaching. Teachers are busy professionals and often do not have the time to continually search through the Internet looking for new educational tools to use in their teaching. Further, it can be difficult to find these tools; the Internet is full of them, but it is hard to know where to look. Compounding all of this, school districts too often do not provide sufficient training or updating on teaching with technology.** <u>The purpose of this essay, then, is to offer teachers a focused look at ten web-based technology tools that they can use to teach social studies.</u>

You probably noticed that, like the first two examples, I create a context (in bold) and I write a thesis sentence (underlined). But unlike the other examples, I do not elaborate on the topic sentence. This is because I use the next paragraph to do that. Here's what it looks like:

> **Teachers often struggle to integrate computer technology into their teaching. Teachers are busy professionals and often do not have the time to continually search through the Internet looking for new educational tools to use in their teaching. Further, it can be difficult to find these tools; the Internet is full of them, but it is hard to know where to look. Compounding all of this, school districts too often do not provide sufficient training or updating on teaching with technology.** <u>The purpose of this essay, then, is to offer teachers a focused look at ten web-based technology tools that they can use to teach social studies.</u>
>
> *Most of these tools are free, and they can be used for a wide range of teaching and learning purposes. Before we examine them, however, let us take a moment to consider what these purposes might be. There are plenty of websites that allow teachers to create flashcards or spelling exercises, such as*

"flashcardmachine.com" and "edhelper.com." Such didactic practice can serve a useful purpose, but the Internet also offers much more. Besides serving as a content resource, now teachers can use tools available on the Internet to help students organize and present information in a variety of engaging and thought-provoking ways. Students can create products such as presentations, timelines, and graphic organizers that include text, images, web links, and video clips. They can create cartoon depictions that explain or illustrate concepts. They can create narrated demonstrations of processes or events. They can even create their own picture storybooks.

The second paragraph continues the introduction by explaining in more detail the purpose of the paper. Notice that I again give readers a sense of what they'll be reading about. I even add a compare/contrast to help make my case; it's in sentences 3 and 4.

What You Should Take Away from These Examples

The structure of the writing is similar for all three "types" of essays. I use different language in each essay, of course, and I make different points. But the order of the introductions is the same, and I achieve the same goals. Also, in each "type" of essay, I just got to the point in each introduction. Nothing fancy; nothing frivolous. Do the same in your writing. I hope this begins to show you that different "types" of essays are actually more similar than they are different, and that these steps will work for all "types" of essays.

Let me make two more important points here. First, some teachers tell students to put the thesis sentence as either the first or the last sentence in your introduction. I think that's a mistake. If I put it first, where do I set up the context? How will readers understand what I'm writing about? If I put it last, where do I tell readers the points I'm going to discuss in the essay? I recommend using the order I'm giving you here: first- set up the context for your essay; second- state your thesis sentence; and third- give readers a sense of the points you're going to discuss in the essay. I do it this way in my published writing; you should too.

Second, you might have noticed that, in the example from the "critical analysis" essay, I used a quotation. That is, I used a sentence from a different article (which

I cited) as support. This is one of many ways to create a context for your essay. I explain citations in detail at the end of the book. What you should learn from this example is that citations are one way of establishing context. You don't necessarily need to use them; I didn't use them in the other two examples. But you do need to use information that you have researched about your topic to help set up the context for readers. What is your topic about? What is going on with that topic that is important for readers to know?

Apply this to Our Sample Essay

Let's turn back to our sample essay. Remember our list of possible body paragraphs? I'll list it below:

> Body paragraph 1: Standardized testing
> Body paragraph 2: Lack of time
> > Pressure to teach facts
> Body paragraph 3: Does it even count?
> > Schools focus on reading, etc
> Body paragraph 4: Too much content
> Body paragraph 5: Lack of resources

I want to write an introduction that establishes the context, clearly states the thesis sentence, and encompasses all of these points. Try this paragraph:

> Teaching social studies is hard. Teachers face a variety of obstacles that can make their job feel impossible. Standardized testing creates significant pressure on teachers. State and school district curriculum plans often ask too much of teachers and students: teach and learn too much content in a too short time frame. This lack of time can pressure teachers to teach just facts. Sometimes social studies isn't tested, so it gets ignored for tested subjects that "matter." Even when social studies is tested, those scores do not always fully count towards a school's accountability rating. Further, teachers often face a lack of resources to meaningfully teach Social Studies.

Can you identify the three sections that we need? Here they are. Remember that **bold** means context, <u>underlined</u> means thesis sentence, and *italics* means points that will be discussed in the essay:

> **Teaching social studies is hard.** <u>Teachers face a variety of obstacles that can make their job feel impossible.</u> *Standardized testing creates significant pressure on teachers. State and school district curriculum plans often ask too much of teachers and students: teach and learn too much content in a too short time frame. This lack of time can pressure teachers to teach just facts. Sometimes social studies isn't tested, so it gets ignored for tested subjects that "matter." Even when social studies is tested, those scores do not always fully count towards a school's accountability rating. Further, teachers often face a lack of resources to meaningfully teach Social Studies.*

In this introduction, I don't need much to set up the context. This is because the points that I briefly discuss will set up the context for me. I just need to mention that teaching is hard. I changed the thesis sentence so that it is a bit more specific, but it essentially means the same thing as the one I initially came up with. And I spend several sentences briefly describing the points I will examine in the essay. How do I know what points I'm going to make in the essay? I've already written topic sentences for each of the paragraphs; I'll just include information from those topic sentences. So let's add this introduction to our developing essay:

<u>Essay Topic</u>: "The difficulty of teaching Social Studies in elementary classrooms"

<u>Introduction</u>: Teaching social studies is hard. Teachers face a variety of obstacles that can make their job feel impossible. Standardized testing creates significant pressure on teachers. State and school district curriculum plans often ask too much of teachers and students: teach and learn too much content in a too short time frame. This lack of time can pressure teachers to teach just facts. Sometimes social studies isn't tested, so it gets ignored for tested subjects that "matter." Even when social studies is tested, those scores do not always fully count towards a school's accountability rating. Further, teachers often face a lack of resources to meaningfully teach Social Studies.

Body paragraph 1
> Topic sentence: Standardized testing shapes, and often limits, how Social Studies is taught.

Body paragraph 2
> Topic sentence: Standardized testing often creates an intense pressure to teach just facts.

Body paragraph 3
> Topic sentence: The focus on tested subjects can de-emphasize Social Studies, since it often is not tested.

Body paragraph 4
> Topic sentence: The sprawling nature of Social Studies content can also impact how it is taught.

Body paragraph 5
> Topic sentence: Finally, a lack of resources can strain Social Studies teaching.

Now it's your turn. Follow the model I'm giving you here and write an introduction to your essay. Be sure that your introduction sets up the context, clearly states the thesis, and gives readers a sense of the points you'll be making in the body of the paper. Don't use complicated language; it's better to be clear and direct.

STEP 5: MAKE YOUR CASE

Now we're going to write the body paragraphs of our essay. You make your case in these paragraphs – you make a convincing, well-supported argument for your reader. You want to gather together all of the facts, reasoning, and other evidence to put into this section in order to best make your case.

Different Ways to Make your Case

There are a lot of different ways to organize this section. In fact, here is where the main differences between various "types" of essays come up. When we write an expository essay or a persuasive essay, for example, we are trying to accomplish specific, yet different things. With the expository essay, we're trying to explain something or analyze something; with the persuasive essay, we're trying to convince readers to agree with us. So, we might use different types of arguments or different structures depending on what we're trying to accomplish with our writing. All this really means is just that we write for different purposes, and the form of our writing will reflect our purpose for writing.

Perhaps the most crucial point I can make here, and what many students find frustrating, is that there really is no best way of organizing your argument in your body paragraphs. If a particular assignment calls for a certain type of argument, such as compare and contrast, then use that, of course. But different types of organization can often work equally well within the same essay – it all depends on how you support your points. For example, I can make a persuasive essay using compare/contrast (by comparing/contrasting reasons to do one thing and not do another), just as effectively as I can by asking and answering questions about whether or not to do something. It all depends on how you put it together. I recommend that you stick with the method that feels most comfortable to you, or with the method that you understand best. There is no formula for this; you'll just have to practice with it.

In this step, I give you three examples of different ways to make arguments and organize information in your body paragraphs. Note that, like the previous step, we aren't working on our sample essay right now. Right now I'm going to show you three different ways of making your case within the body paragraphs of an essay. At the end of this step, we'll apply these ideas and principles to our sample essay.

Compare and Contrast

One way to organize and analyze your points is through compare and contrast. Compare/contrast works well if you are discussing at least two different examples, concepts, etc. Compare/contrast helps you to make your case by offering examples and non-examples of your points. Read the paragraph below:

> <u>Defining quality in teaching is unusually difficult.</u> **Were anyone serious about this issue, they would soon realize that quality is an ineffable concept, as the best-selling book by Pirsig (1974) made clear. Defining quality always requires value judgments about which disagreements abound.** *Studying teaching cross-culturally makes this evident (Alexander, 2000). A high-quality teacher in India does not allow questioning by students. Students simply listen for hours on end. The opposite is true in many American classes, where students are expected to raise questions during class. Alexander (2000) found that maintaining discipline is not part of any definition of quality in Russia or India because there are almost no discipline problems in their schools. But in the organizationally complex world of American and British schools, with individualization of some activities, promotion of collaboration and negotiation, and a concern for students' feelings, there is a greater incidence of behavior problems. Thus, American and British teachers of high quality must have classroom management skills that are unnecessary in Russia or India.* (Berliner, 2005)

Let's break down this paragraph; it's different than most of the other paragraphs we've looked at. This paragraph compares and contrasts schools in Russia and India with schools in America and Great Britain. But notice that the author doesn't just jump into the compare and contrast. The author first sets up what's going to happen. The author begins with the topic sentence, which is underlined. The next two sentences, in bold, provide context, in this case more explanation of the topic sentence. The first sentence that is italicized sets up the compare and contrast. The rest of the paragraph, also in italics, contains the compare and contrast. Let's look more closely at the sentences in italics.

The first two sentences are about schools in India, specifically that students are not allowed to ask questions in class: "A high-quality teacher in India does not allow questioning by students. Students simply listen for hours on end." Then the author compares/contrasts that point with the fact that American classes expect students to ask questions: "The opposite is true in many American classes, where students are expected to raise questions during class." The author then moves to the next point of comparison – maintaining discipline in the different classrooms: "Alexander (2000) found that maintaining discipline is not part of any definition of quality in Russia or India because there are almost no discipline problems in their schools." This sentence focuses on discipline in Russia and India. The next sentence compares/contrasts with discipline in American schools: "But in the organizationally complex world of American and British schools, with individualization of some activities, promotion of collaboration and negotiation, and a concern for students' feelings, there is a greater incidence of behavior problems." The last sentence of the paragraph provides a small concluding thought about this specific point regarding classroom management. Compare and contrast is set up like this for all essays. Decide which specific points you want to compare/contrast, then present information in a "back-and-forth" that compares/contrasts these specific points, just like this author did, to make your argument.

Question and Answer
Another way of arranging your argument is by question and answer. In this method, you simply ask one or more questions and then proceed to provide answers to those questions. This method helps to focus your readers' attention through the question and answer process. The method makes it easy to address your points, and the questions often create the context for you, but the risk is that your essay will read like a list and not like a discussion. Here's an example below. The first two sentences (in bold) pose the questions. The topic sentence (underlined) frames an answer for the questions, and the rest of the paragraph (in italics) offers more specific answers to the questions:

But what do we know about Socrates and the method he used to interrogate Athenians in the agora? And what are we talking about when we call it the "Socratic method?" <u>As it turns out, we may be</u>

mistaking common phrasing for common practice. After all, classrooms in which the Socratic method is ostensibly employed are hardly all the same. Teachers are at the center of some and at the periphery of others. Talk is common in all, but it includes chaotic zigzagging in one class and linear directionality in another. Socratic classrooms can be relaxed or tense, loud or quiet, large or small. They can, in other words, seem as different from each other as they seem from classes in which other methods are the basis of instruction. (Schneider, 2012)

Question and answer is a more direct way of structuring your argument than compare/contrast. It works well when you're discussing just one thing. You just state the question(s) you want to answer and then go about answering that question. It's pretty straightforward. One advantage to this method is that the questions you ask will set up the context for you. Notice what the author tells you in the questions: that they are about Socrates; that he used a particular method; that he used this method to interrogate people from Athens; and that we call it the "Socratic method." That's a lot of information that will help your readers understand what you are discussing. Think about how much less information is provided by a similar question: "What is the "Socratic method?" This second question gives readers much less context. So, it is important for you to remember to write questions that give readers lots of information.

Point by Point

Perhaps the most well-known way of making an argument is to list your points one by one. This method is similar to the "Question and Answer" format, except that you don't begin with questions. You still need to provide context to your readers, however. The difficulty with this method is stating a general point that you then discuss in detail. Read this example paragraph:

> **The first part of the outcomes trap is equating both pupils' learning and teacher quality with test scores. Increasingly, under the current educational regime, this is the case.** <u>This equation is far too simplistic a way to conceptualize the complexities of teaching and learning.</u> *Teaching does not simply involve transmitting bits of information that can be tested, and learning is not just receiving information about subject matter. Both are far more complex. In addition, schools and teacher education programs have purposes in addition to pupils' academic learning,*

including their social and emotional development and their ability to participate in a democratic society. To represent all of the complex aspects involved in teacher quality and pupils' learning in one number derived from increases in achievement test scores is a trap – it reflects impoverished notions of teaching and learning not at all in keeping with research or experience in these areas and ignores broader commitments. (Cochran-Smith, 2005)

The first two sentences, in bold, provide context. They tell readers that the paragraph will be discussing the "outcomes trap" and how that relates to learning, teacher quality, and test scores. And they tell us that the paragraph is referring to the present (the "*current* educational regime"). The underlined sentence is the topic sentence. It tells readers that the usual way of determining teacher quality (through students' test scores) is too simple. The rest of the paragraph, in italics, states a number of points that make the case for why test scores cannot account for the complexities of teaching and learning.

What These Methods All Have in Common

Did you notice what these different ways of making your case have in common? First, they all give the reader a context for understanding the argument, and they do this in the first few sentences. Without this context, readers will be less likely to understand the points you are trying to make. Second, each type of paragraph has a topic sentence, towards the beginning of the paragraph (and often as the first sentence of the paragraph), that identifies what the argument will be. And third, each type of paragraph spends most of the paragraph presenting points that make the case. The importance of these points can't be overemphasized. Put simply, you should do these three things: 1) tell your reader the general context for your paragraph, 2) get to your point as soon as possible, and 3) elaborate that point. Did you notice how each of the example paragraphs above clearly stated the topic sentence and established the context first (the bold and underlined sentences) and then spent most of the paragraph supporting the topic (the sentences in italics)? You should do this too. Students often want to move on too quickly from a paragraph and get to the next idea. That's a mistake. You need to fully explain/defend/support your topic sentence. In these paragraphs, it's always better to write more rather than write less. How do you support your topic sentence? Well, that's where your research and your thinking come in. Basically, you need to offer enough supporting details that go with the topic of that sentence. Use the three examples above as models. They all make complex arguments, but they do it in different ways. You'll just need to practice; there's no other way around it.

Apply this to Our Sample Essay

We'll now apply this to our sample essay. Let's review what we have so far. Remember that we can keep changing things (thesis sentence, introduction, topic sentences, paragraph order, etc) until we find what we like.

Topic: The difficulty of teaching social studies

Introduction: Teaching social studies is hard. Teachers face a variety of obstacles that can make their job feel impossible. Standardized testing creates significant pressure on teachers. State and school district curriculum plans often ask too much of teachers and students: teach and learn too much content in a too short time frame. This lack of time can pressure teachers to teach just facts. Sometimes social studies isn't tested, so it gets ignored for tested subjects that "matter." Even when social studies is tested, those scores do not always fully count towards a school's accountability rating. Further, teachers often face a lack of resources to meaningfully teach Social Studies.

Paragraph: Standardized testing shapes, and often limits, how Social Studies is taught.

Paragraph: Standardized testing often creates an intense pressure to teach just facts.

Paragraph: The focus on tested subjects can de-emphasize Social Studies, since it often is not tested.

Paragraph: The sprawling nature of Social Studies content can also impact how it is taught.

Paragraph: Finally, a lack of resources can strain Social Studies teaching.

Ok. Now we're going to fill out our body paragraphs. Remember what I wrote earlier about continually changing or revising your essay as you continue to put it together? Well, you're about to see an example of it. I've been working with a certain plan for my essay; I've developed some paragraph ideas and topic sentences to go with them. But, as I worked on this section, I realized that I needed to make some big changes to my paragraph topics and topic sentences. I found another way to do it that works better. So, when you read through the new body paragraphs, you'll see some changes. I'll explain the changes at the end of this section.

I underlined the thesis and topic sentences. And I put in **bold** any sentences that create context for readers. The rest of the sentences, in *italics*, support/explain/defend the topic sentence in each paragraph (just like the italicized sentences did in the examples above):

Introduction: **Teaching social studies is hard.** Teachers face a variety of obstacles that can make their job feel impossible. *Standardized testing creates significant pressure on teachers. State and school district curriculum plans often ask too much of teachers and students: teach and learn too much content in too short of a time frame. This lack of time can pressure teachers to teach just facts. Sometimes social studies isn't tested, so it gets ignored for tested subjects that "matter." Yet, even when Social Studies is tested, those scores do not always fully count towards a school's accountability rating. Models of quality teaching can also be in short supply in Social Studies. Further, teachers often face a lack of resources to meaningfully teach Social Studies.*

Paragraph: **Teachers constantly struggle with a lack of time to teach.** Standardized testing plays a crucial role in this time problem. *When Social Studies is not tested, it tends* *to get ignored. Elementary schools routinely allot as little as 45 minutes a week to Social Studies. What meaningful teaching and learning can happen in only 45 minutes a week? Middle and high schools allow more scheduled time, but frequently subtract from that time by scheduling things such as pep rallies, school assemblies, and fundraising meetings during Social Studies classes. These practices send a clear picture to students that Social Studies, when it is not tested, is less important to the school than tested subjects.*

Paragraph: <u>When Social Studies is tested, teachers face a different problem: too much to teach in the time they have.</u> *This often leads teachers to engage in "inch deep and mile wide" teaching practices. Compounding this time problem is the fact that students usually come to Social Studies with little to no familiarity with the content. Teachers then spend considerable time on repetitive, "drill and kill" teaching practices in the hope they will help students to retain information at least until testing day. While many teachers would like to engage students in more meaningful activities, they often do not feel they have time for it. According to one high school history teacher in a study by Kenneth Vogler (2005),*

> *I use the entire academic year preparing my students for the United States history subject exam. My choice of instructional delivery and materials is completely dependent on preparation for this test. Therefore, I do not use current events, long-term projects, or creative group/corporate work because this is not tested and the delivery format is not used. All my tests reflect the testing format of the subject area tests — multiple-choice and open ended questions (p. 19).*

Some researchers claim that mandated accountability exams lead to a "just the facts, ma'am" approach to teaching social studies (Vogler & Virtue, 2007). Other researchers go further and contend that "because multiple-choice testing leads to multiple-choice teaching, the methods that teachers have in their arsenal become reduced, and teaching work is deskilled" (Smith, 1991, p. 10).

Paragraph: <u>Another reason Social Studies is hard to teach is that teachers have so few models of good Social Studies teaching.</u> *Most Social Studies teaching takes the form of "telling," in which teachers lecture, i.e. "tell" students information, perhaps show a picture or video, and then test students on the content. In this paradigm, students are not asked to actively learn, only to passively retain information. There is a simple reason for this: teachers usually teach the way they were taught when they were students. High schools and universities are notorious for this kind of passive teaching and learning. So, it makes sense that teachers continue to use these methods. The problem is that they just don't work that well if thinking is the goal.*

Paragraph: <u>Lastly, finding and using quality resources presents an ongoing challenge to Social Studies teachers.</u> *Textbooks are the most commonly used resource. This makes sense. Almost all classrooms have them, and they present information through efficient explanations, pictures, charts, and other visual methods. And teachers do not need to go looking for them, which may be the biggest benefit of all. Yet, textbooks contain a number of problems too: they usually present surface-level understandings; their reading level is often too high for students; and they always contain unaddressed bias. Further, and perhaps most important, they do a bad job of presenting multiple perspectives about issues and events. Teachers, then, need to find resources on their own that can offer students more depth and more varied perspectives. These other types of resources exist. Libraries and museums will often loan entire boxes of varied materials to teachers. Nonprofits and NGOs sometimes provide materials about specific topics. And the Internet, of course, is awash in historical information. The challenge for teachers is creating the time to acquire these resources and learning how to use them, especially when teachers are so often overwhelmed by the other responsibilities of their jobs.*

Did you spot the changes? I changed the order of the paragraphs some, and I changed some of the topics of the paragraphs. I even went from 5 body paragraphs to 4 body paragraphs, because I decided that "sprawling content" in what was body paragraph #4 should be put with the discussion of time in body paragraph #2 (the one about teachers having too much to teach). Since I changed the order and content of the paragraphs, I also had to change the introduction some. I made these changes because I think they better support the thesis statement than what I originally had written. I'm showing you this because I want you to feel free to make changes to your essay in order to keep improving it. Your essay is only finished (or "final") when you decide to stop working on it.

I make most of my argument in these new paragraphs using the "Point by Point" format. For example, look at the second body paragraph. I state the topic in the first sentence. Every sentence after that is a point that supports the topic. You'll also notice that I use quotes for support. If you have quotes that work, that's how you use them. We'll go into detail about how to use quotations in the bonus section at the end of the book. For now, just know that I can use quotes as effective support. But I don't use the quote by itself; the quote illustrates a point I made in the previous sentence.

In addition to "Point by Point" style, I also use "Question and Answer" and "Compare/Contrast" some. In the first body paragraph, I ask the question, "What meaningful teaching and learning can happen in only 45 min a week?" Then I address the question. That question also responds to points I made earlier in that paragraph. In the last body paragraph, I do a short "Compare/Contrast" about the positive and negative aspects of textbooks. Let's take a closer look at the last paragraph. After the topic sentence, I note the positive things about textbooks. The sixth sentence, the one that begins with "Yet," shows the contrast. I use that sentence and the next two sentences explaining the bad things about textbooks. Then I make the point, using "point by point" style, to explain ways that teachers can find quality resources to use while teaching. I want you to see that it's ok for you to use multiple ways of making your case, just as long as each paragraph has a clear focus on only one idea, which we're going to address in the next step.

One last note, remember that if you use or reference information from specific sources, you need to cite it. We want to avoid plagiarism. Plus, citations add weight to our essay. I know the information in our sample essay from my work in schools, so I don't need to cite it. But I did cite two articles in paragraph 3, because I used sentences and details from those articles. Be sure that you do the same.

STEP 6: ENSURE YOUR BODY PARAGRAPHS ARE FOCUSED

Now that you've written your body paragraphs, let's do some housekeeping and make sure those paragraphs are as focused as they can be. A big mistake that students often make is putting too many ideas into one paragraph. I'm going to show you some examples of paragraphs that are vague and lack focus, and I'm going to show you how to fix those problems. I want you to remember these four things from Step 6:

1. Paragraphs need to focus on only one topic.
2. The topic sentence clearly states that topic.
3. All other sentences in the paragraph support or explain that topic.
4. When you change to a new idea, begin a new paragraph.

Now, if you've written strong and clear topic sentences, you're well on your way to creating focused paragraphs. But problems can still come up, so it's better to be sure. We'll start with an example of a paragraph a student wrote that has too many ideas crammed into it. Read the following paragraph and try to identify the main idea:

> In the SAGE journals, "Bilingual Classroom Studies," there are questions and issues that underline bilingual education are constrained by deficit views about the abilities and experiences of language minority students. However there is a lot of research that has emphasized how well students acquire English, assimilate into mainstream culture, and perform on tests of basic skills. Employing a sociocultural perspective that acknowledges the many resources that are available to children outside of the school. The author describes how research about children's communities can be used to enhance instruction because I also believe that the community plays a huge role in student's education. In order for this to happen I believe teachers need to redefine their roles so that they can collaborate and work together to focus on ways to bring about educational change.

Could you identify a main idea? At first, this paragraph seems like it might work. It references a journal article in providing context for readers. Then it seems to establish a compare/contrast in the next sentence (with the word "However"). But then the paragraph keeps introducing new topics, at least as I see it. I'll number them for you:

> (#1) In the SAGE journals, "Bilingual Classroom Studies," there are questions and issues that underline bilingual education are constrained by deficit views about the abilities and experiences of language minority students. (#2) However there is a lot of research that has emphasized how well students acquire English, assimilate into mainstream culture, and perform on tests of basic skills. (#3) Employing a sociocultural perspective that acknowledges the many resources that are available to children outside of the school. (#4) The author describes how research about children's communities can be used to enhance instruction because I also believe that the community plays a huge role in student's education. (#5) In order for this to happen I believe teachers need to redefine their roles so that they can collaborate and work together to focus on ways to bring about educational change.

The first sentence (#1) seems to create a topic about "deficit views about the abilities and experiences of language minority children." But then the second sentence (#2) offers more ideas, this time about students acquiring English, assimilating into mainstream culture, and performing on tests. The third sentence (#3) offers even more ideas, something about employing a sociocultural perspective. The fourth sentence (#4) moves to children's communities. Finally, the fifth sentence (#5) adds "teachers redefining their roles" to this assortment of ideas. This is a huge array of ideas within this paragraph! Obviously, this is a problem. But it's one that students often make.

The following paragraph, from a different student's writing, is another example of what *not* to do. Just like I did in the paragraph above, I also number the ideas in this next paragraph:

> (#1) Some of the challenges for ELL students in the mainstream social studies classrooms encounters a number of critical barriers which may impede their citizenship education. Some of the barriers include the ELL students lack of prior exposure to elementary school social studies curriculum, a rudimentary understanding of the cultural context in which social studies knowledge in constructed, and more importantly, their lack

of English literacy skills which are vital not only for comprehending social studies material but also for acculturation and socialization in the dominant culture (Haynes, 2005). (#2) Teaching ELL students in mainstream high school social studies classrooms poses a challenge to the social studies teachers who derive their content from history, political science, sociology, geology, and economics, each one of which contains its own specialized jargon and concepts rooted in American culture. (#3) Cultural literacy poses a unique challenge for both teacher and student in the ELL social studies classroom. Teachers may or may not be familiar with the cultures students bring with them to the classroom, and students are often unfamiliar with both the content knowledge and the rituals of their newly adopted culture. In the mainstream social studies course, ELL students are expected to learn about the society, history, economy, and political system of their newly adopted country. Although it would be erroneous to assume that ELL students have no prior knowledge about the United States, it is apt to think that their experiences with American culture are limited and /or potentially skewed according to the views of their home culture and home educational system. (#4)In addition, learning social studies lessons requires proficiency in reading and writing in English language. Deborah J. Short (1994) suggests that "Social studies is closely bound to literacy skills" (p. 36). Literacy skills for social studies includes reading, writing, speaking, researching, and organizing information in English. I believe this is something I completely agree with because social studies does have to a lot with literacy skills.

This paragraph begins with what seems like a single idea (even though the wording needs work): barriers which impede citizenship education (#1). The next sentence even begins with "some barriers include," which should be a good start. It tells readers that a detailed discussion of barriers is coming next. But then the student switches to high school (#2). The student then references cultural literacy (#3), which is mentioned in the beginning of the paragraph. But the skip from elementary school to high school is jarring; I'm not sure if the author is now referring to elementary school or high school (or both). Finally, there's one more skip, this time to literacy skills (#4). By the time I get to the end of the paragraph, we are a long way away from citizenship education. What the student should have done is clearly list what the barriers to citizenship education are, assuming that's the purpose of the paragraph, and then discuss each of those barriers: what are they, how do they fit together, how do they impede learning?

Now let's examine two examples of paragraphs *that are* clear and focused. Actually, you've already seen them. Here's the first one:

> Defining **quality** in teaching is unusually difficult. Were anyone serious about this issue, they would soon realize that **quality** is an ineffable concept, as the best-selling book by Pirsig (1974) made clear. Defining **quality** always requires value judgments about which disagreements abound. Studying teaching cross-culturally makes this evident (Alexander, 2000). A high-**quality** teacher in India does not allow questioning by students. Students simply listen for hours on end. The opposite is true in many American classes, where students are expected to raise questions during class. Alexander (2000) found that maintaining discipline is not part of any definition of **quality** in Russia or India because there are almost no discipline problems in their schools. But in the organizationally complex world of American and British schools, with individualization of some activities, promotion of collaboration and negotiation, and a concern for students' feelings, there is a greater incidence of behavior problems. Thus, American and British teachers of high **quality** must have classroom management skills that are unnecessary in Russia or India. (Berliner, 2005)

I used this paragraph earlier to demonstrate compare/contrast. Here, we can see how the topic remains clear: it's about "quality." All of the examples refer back to quality. The author uses a book reference about quality. And the author repeatedly uses the word "quality" throughout the paragraph.

Here's another example of a focused paragraph:

> The first part of the outcomes trap is equating both pupils' learning and teacher quality with test scores. Increasingly, under the current educational regime, this is the case. This equation is far too simplistic a way to conceptualize the complexities of teaching and learning. Teaching does not simply involve transmitting bits of information that can be tested, and learning is not just receiving information about subject matter. Both are far more complex. In addition, schools and teacher education programs have purposes in addition to pupils' academic learning, including their social and emotional development and their ability to participate in a democratic society. To represent all of the complex aspects involved in teacher quality and pupils' learning in one

number derived from increases in achievement test scores is a trap – it reflects impoverished notions of teaching and learning not at all in keeping with research or experience in these areas and ignores broader commitments. (Cochran-Smith, 2005)

We saw this paragraph earlier as well. Look at it again in terms of focus. The topic of the paragraph is about how test scores are too simplistic to capture the complexities of teaching. This is established in the first few sentences. The rest of the paragraph offers examples of complexities of teaching. The last sentence in the paragraph sums up the argument against using test scores to measure the complexity of teaching. Now you've seen examples of paragraphs that have too many ideas in them, and you've seen examples of paragraphs that are focused. In our sample essay, there is only one main idea per paragraph. Now apply this analysis to the paragraphs in your essay and make sure that you only have one idea per paragraph.

STEP 7: CONCLUDE WITH PURPOSE

Earlier, I told you that the introduction to an essay should accomplish three specific things. With conclusions, however, you're really trying to do just one thing – make your point stick. This is your last opportunity to give readers something to think about, to make whatever big-picture point you're trying to make. In other words, you don't just end, you end with a specific purpose. Sometimes you might want to restate the main points from your essay – that's probably the most common way that students will end essays. But other times you might want to do something else: maybe interpret your points, maybe show how your points apply to something else, maybe leave your readers with some sort of question. There are many options; you just need to decide what you want to do with it.

Remember a few things when writing a conclusion. You don't necessarily need a topic sentence. Instead, you will transition into your conclusion with a sentence that feels like you are wrapping it up. Try not to write "In conclusion;" there are more artful ways of finishing. Don't introduce new information or new details; that should be done in the body paragraphs. Don't go on and on about any one particular point; a conclusion should address your entire argument/paper, not elaborate specific points. Some things you might want to do are to return to points you made in your introduction and to leave your reader with something to think about.

I'll show you three examples of effective conclusions and explain to you what I was trying to do with those conclusions. Conclusions only make sense in relation to introductions, so I'll have to show you both an introduction paragraph and a conclusion paragraph to different essays. These examples are taken from articles that I published in scholarly journals. Notice in these examples how I tie the introductions and conclusions together and I try to leave readers with a thought to consider:

Example #1: I make a connection to other research findings:

> *Introduction:* After decades of research, the nature of the impact of state-mandated accountability testing on teachers'

classroom practices remains contested. Many researchers argue that teachers change their teaching in response to mandated testing. Yet, other researchers contend that the nature and degree of the impact of testing on teaching remains unclear. Some researchers maintain that teachers' views on subject matter and on learners, as well as local schooling contexts plays a role in shaping teaching practices that might be as or more powerful that testing influences. Most researchers, however, claim a deleterious impact of testing on classroom teaching.

Conclusion: This study offers support for the argument that the influence state-mandated testing has on classroom teaching depends on how teachers interpret state testing and let it guide their actions. Even though mandated accountability exams can cause teachers to feel pressured by test-related time and coverage concerns, they are not necessarily limited to "multiple-choice" teaching. Perhaps ironically, instead of causing teachers to become deskilled, if teachers are to engage their students in deep and meaningful learning, to teach *beyond* the test, they will need to use all of their skills to negotiate the hurdles that mandated testing can erect in the path of those learning goals.

Example #2: I make a case for the benefits educators can receive from the argument in the essay:

Introduction: Labels seem to be an inherent part of education. The broad generalizations captured by labels such as *ELL, at-risk, special ed,* and *GT* both illuminate and guide how educators think about, talk about, and implement educational concepts and practices. Many scholars investigate the effects of labeling on students and society. Less considered, however, is the relationship between the use of labels and how educators think about teaching and curriculum. Yet, when considering new styles of instruction, educators can benefit from *rethinking* two commonly used labels in education: "teacher-centered" and "student-centered."

Conclusion: As educators rethink old instructional methods and develop new ones, reconsidering the labels used to describe educational contexts does not simply clarify educational vernacular. It helps us to more carefully evaluate both new and everyday teaching structures and strategies. It helps us to more clearly consider and articulate how educational perspectives manifest in schools and classrooms. It helps us to gain precision in our research design, analysis, and conclusions. And it carves a space that recognizes an essential distinction between "student-facilitated" and "student-centered" contexts. Expanding the labels we use to categorize educational contexts to "teacher-centered," "student-centered," and "student-facilitated" helps us to more productively value and promote a paradigmatic quality towards which many educators aspire.

Example #3: I argue for what we should do with the information presented in the essay:

Introduction: The practice of having students read textbooks aloud in class, commonly known as "round robin reading," is much maligned. Indeed, some researchers argue that round robin reading can probably be considered one of the most harmful components of group learning. Yet, despite the widespread and intense criticism, teachers across the country continue to use round robin reading in their classrooms. This begs a question: why is a practice that is so routinely criticized so commonly used? This article offers insight into this question in the context of three middle school social studies teachers' classrooms. Contrary to being a harmful component of learning, in these classrooms round robin reading works as a productive teaching tool that helps teachers to enact a variety of purposes: it helps teachers to explain specific concepts, it provides a context for notetaking and questioning, and it serves as a "jumping off" point for lecture.

Conclusion: These findings hold implications for teachers' professional development. Round robin reading is certainly used unproductively in classrooms. But as this study shows, round robin reading does not have to be ineffective teaching practice. The literature clearly shows that teachers continue to use round robin reading despite efforts to halt its use. While much effort is made to eliminate round robin reading, almost no effort seems to be made to help teachers learn to use it wisely and effectively. Teacher education and professional development can help with that. There is no need to eliminate this practice; instead, we need to help teachers learn to use it well.

Apply This to Our Sample Essay

I'll add a conclusion to what we've already been working on. Let's compare our existing introduction with this new conclusion:

Introduction: Teaching social studies is hard. Teachers face a variety of obstacles that can make their job feel impossible. Standardized testing creates significant pressure on teachers. State and school district curriculum plans often ask too much of teachers and students: teach and learn too much content in too short of a time frame. This lack of time can pressure teachers to teach just facts. Sometimes social studies isn't tested, so it gets ignored for tested subjects that "matter." Yet, even when Social Studies is tested, those scores do not always fully count towards a school's accountability rating. Models of quality teaching can also be in short supply in Social Studies. Further, teachers often face a lack of resources to meaningfully teach Social Studies.

Conclusion: Even with all of these challenges, quality teaching in Social Studies is crucial. Social Studies helps to create a public that is literate about social and historical issues, can analyze problems through context, and has a global awareness of the challenges facing society. To create such a public, students must be presented with meaningful problems and asked to engage in analytical thinking. Forty-five minutes a week of Social Studies won't cut it, nor will a reductionist focus on test scores or teaching methods that keep students disengaged. Teachers face significant challenges in teaching Social Studies. But the urgency to confront those challenges in order to create this much needed public has never been greater.

The whole essay is about the challenges to teaching Social Studies. So, it makes sense to begin the conclusion with a reference to those challenges. Then I argue why Social Studies is important. Next, I refer to some of the teaching methods that teachers should use. I end the conclusion by repeating my reference to the challenges in teaching Social Studies and that it is crucial to meet those challenges. Let's see what the whole essay now looks like:

Teaching social studies is hard. Teachers face a variety of obstacles that can make their job feel impossible. Standardized testing creates significant pressure on teachers. State and school district curriculum plans often ask too much of teachers and students: teach and learn too much content in too short of a time frame. This lack of time can pressure teachers to teach just facts. Sometimes social studies isn't tested, so it gets ignored for tested subjects that "matter." Yet, even when Social Studies is tested, those scores do not always fully count towards a school's accountability rating. Models of quality teaching can also be in short supply in Social Studies. Further, teachers often face a lack of resources to meaningfully teach Social Studies.

Teachers constantly struggle with a lack of time to teach. Standardized testing plays a crucial role in this time problem. When Social Studies is not tested, it tends to get ignored. Elementary schools routinely allot as little as 45 minutes a week to Social Studies. What meaningful teaching and learning can happen in only 45 minutes a week? Middle and high schools allow more scheduled time, but frequently subtract from that time by scheduling things such as pep rallies, school assemblies, and fundraising meetings during Social Studies classes. These practices send a clear picture to students that Social Studies, when it is not tested, is less important to the school than tested subjects.

When Social Studies is tested, teachers face a different problem: too much to teach in the time they have. This often leads teachers to engage in "inch deep and mile wide" teaching practices. Compounding this time problem is the fact that students usually come to Social Studies with little to no familiarity with the content. Teachers then spend considerable time on repetitive, "drill and kill" teaching practices in the hope they will help students to retain information at least until testing day. While many teachers would like to engage students in more meaningful activities, they often do not feel they have time for it. According to one high school history teacher in a study by Kenneth Vogler (2005),

> I use the entire academic year preparing my students for the United States history subject exam. My choice of instructional delivery and materials is completely dependent on preparation for this test. Therefore, I do not use current events, long-term projects, or creative group/corporate work because this is not tested and the delivery format is not used. All my tests reflect the testing format of the subject area tests – multiple-choice and open ended questions (p. 19).

Some researchers claim that mandated accountability exams lead to a "just the facts, ma'am" approach to teaching social studies (Vogler & Virtue, 2007). Other researchers go further and contend that "because multiple-choice testing leads to multiple-choice teaching, the methods that teachers have in their arsenal become reduced, and teaching work is deskilled" (Smith, 1991, p. 10).

Another reason Social Studies is hard to teach is that teachers have so few models of good Social Studies teaching. Most Social Studies teaching takes the form of "telling," in which teachers lecture, i.e. "tell" students information, perhaps show a picture or video, and then test students on the content. In this paradigm, students are not asked to actively learn, only to passively retain information. There is a simple reason for this: teachers usually teach the way they were taught when they were students. High schools and universities are notorious for this kind of passive teaching and learning. So, it makes sense that teachers continue to use these methods. The problem is that they just don't work that well if thinking is the goal.

Lastly, finding and using quality resources presents an ongoing challenge to Social Studies teachers. Textbooks are the most commonly used resource. This makes sense. Almost all classrooms have them, and they present information through efficient explanations, pictures, charts, and other visual methods. And teachers do not need to go looking for them, which may be the biggest benefit of all. Yet, textbooks contain a number of problems too: they usually present surface-level understandings; their reading level is often too high for students; and they always contain unaddressed bias. Further, and perhaps most important, they do a bad job of presenting multiple perspectives about issues and events. Teachers, then, need to find resources on their own that can offer students more depth and more varied perspectives. These other types of resources exist. Libraries and museums will often loan entire boxes of varied materials to teachers. Nonprofits and NGOs sometimes provide materials about specific topics. And the Internet, of course, is awash in historical information. The challenge for teachers is creating the time to acquire these resources and learning how to use them, especially when teachers are so often overwhelmed by the other responsibilities of their jobs.

Even with all of these challenges, quality teaching in Social Studies is crucial. Social Studies helps to create a public that is literate about social and historical issues, can analyze problems through context, and has a global awareness of the challenges facing society. To create such a public, students must be presented with meaningful problems and asked to engage in analytical thinking. Forty-five minutes a week of Social Studies won't cut it, nor will a reductionist focus on test scores or teaching methods that keep students disengaged. Teachers face significant challenges in teaching Social Studies. But the urgency to confront those challenges in order to create this much needed public has never been greater.

Now it's your turn. Decide how you want to conclude your essay. Perhaps use one of the examples I gave you as a model.

STEP 8: WRITE A POWERFUL FINAL SENTENCE

Now that you've written your conclusion, let's take another look at the last sentence in the conclusion, which is the last sentence in your essay. This final sentence, what I'm going to also call your "closing sentence," is especially important...and especially hard to write. Just as your introduction and conclusion go together, so do your opening and your closing sentence. In your conclusion, you want to make your point stick. You might have restated your main argument or developed a few questions for your readers to think about. Your final sentence, however, presents a more focused challenge. This is because it's the last thing that readers will read in your essay. So it's important that we get this right.

Examples of Final Sentences

The big question here is - how do you make a final impression without being contrived or stale or repetitive? You can use a closing sentence to do a number of things. You can reiterate a persuasive point. You can leave readers with something you want them to think about. You can tie it back to the opening paragraph, as if tying a bow. You can use humor. You can try to make a personal point with readers. Many different forms of closing sentences can be effective. Just be sure to use one that is appropriate for your essay topic. Here are a few examples of closing sentences. I've paired them with the opening sentences in the introductions in their essays so that you can see how the opening and closing sentences fit together.

Use humor:

> Opening sentence: So, what's your teaching method?
> Closing sentence: One can only hope that the ghost of Socrates appreciates irony.

Leave readers with something to think about:

> Opening sentence: After decades of research, the nature of the impact of state-mandated accountability testing on teachers' classroom practices remains contested.

Closing sentence: Perhaps ironically, instead of causing teachers to become deskilled, if teachers are to engage their students in deep and meaningful learning, to teach *beyond* the test, they will need to use all of their skills to negotiate the hurdles that mandated testing can erect in the path of those learning goals.

Reiterate a point:

Opening sentence: "Best practice" would seem to be the pinnacle of practice to generate learning inside the classroom.

Closing sentence: Instead of proclaiming practices that are "best" across a range of educational settings, educators should keep in mind that any "best" practice is the result of a combination of factors and is ultimately a negotiation among teachers, students, and institutional contexts.

Try to persuade the reader:

Opening sentence: Social studies classes can often feel like a timed race over an obstacle course.

Closing sentence: Because they are relatively short and compressed productions and because they lend themselves to a wide range of subjects, "Act it Outs" can be a regular part of any social studies classroom.

Make it practical:

Opening sentence: Teachers often struggle to integrate computer technology into their teaching.

Closing sentence: If the purpose is to have students engage with concepts in creative ways, web-based resources such as these are great tools for teachers and students to use.

We'll now return to our sample essay and take another look at our closing sentence. Notice how the closing sentence reflects the opening sentence. The opening sentence states that teaching Social Studies is hard. The closing sentence refers to the challenges of teaching Social Studies, which is a direct reference to the opening sentence. This gives the essay nice balance between the beginning and ending. Also, the closing sentence tries to emphasize a point about the urgency of addressing those challenges.

Opening sentence: Teaching social studies is hard.
Closing sentence: But the urgency to confront those challenges in order to create this much needed public has never been greater.

I'll paste the whole essay again and **BOLD** the opening sentence and the closing sentence. I will also underline the thesis sentence and all of the topic sentences. This will help you to see the opening and closing sentences in the context of the full essay. Here's what these sentences look like in the essay:

Teaching social studies is hard. <u>Teachers face a variety of obstacles that can make their job feel impossible.</u> Standardized testing creates significant pressure on teachers. State and school district curriculum plans often ask too much of teachers and students: teach and learn too much content in too short of a time frame. This lack of time can pressure teachers to teach just facts. Sometimes social studies isn't tested, so it gets ignored for tested subjects that "matter." Yet, even when Social Studies is tested, those scores do not always fully count towards a school's accountability rating. Models of quality teaching can also be in short supply in Social Studies. Further, teachers often face a lack of resources to meaningfully teach Social Studies.

Teachers constantly struggle with a lack of time to teach. <u>Standardized testing plays a crucial role in this time problem.</u> When Social Studies is not tested, it tends to get ignored. Elementary schools routinely allot as little as 45 minutes a week to Social Studies. What meaningful teaching and learning can happen in only 45 minutes a week? Middle and high schools allow more scheduled time, but frequently subtract from that time by scheduling things such as pep rallies, school assemblies, and fundraising meetings during Social

Studies classes. These practices send a clear picture to students that Social Studies, when it is not tested, is less important to the school than tested subjects.

When Social Studies is tested, teachers face a different problem: too much to teach in the time they have. This often leads teachers to engage in "inch deep and mile wide" teaching practices. Compounding this time problem is the fact that students usually come to Social Studies with little to no familiarity with the content. Teachers then spend considerable time on repetitive, "drill and kill" teaching practices in the hope they will help students to retain information at least until testing day. While many teachers would like to engage students in more meaningful activities, they often do not feel they have time for it. According to one high school history teacher in a study by Kenneth Vogler (2005),

> I use the entire academic year preparing my students for the United States history subject exam. My choice of instructional delivery and materials is completely dependent on preparation for this test. Therefore, I do not use current events, long-term projects, or creative group/corporate work because this is not tested and the delivery format is not used. All my tests reflect the testing format of the subject area tests – multiple-choice and open ended questions (p. 19).

Some researchers claim that mandated accountability exams lead to a "just the facts, ma'am" approach to teaching social studies (Vogler & Virtue, 2007). Other researchers go further and contend that "because multiple-choice testing leads to multiple-choice teaching, the methods that teachers have in their arsenal become reduced, and teaching work is deskilled" (Smith, 1991, p. 10).

Another reason Social Studies is hard to teach is that teachers have so few models of good Social Studies teaching. Most Social Studies teaching takes the form of "telling," in which teachers lecture, i.e. "tell" students information, perhaps show a picture or video, and then test students on the content. In this paradigm, students are not asked to actively learn, only to passively retain information. There is a simple reason for this: teachers usually teach the way they were taught when they were students. High schools and universities are notorious for this kind of passive teaching and learning. So, it makes sense that teachers continue to use these methods. The problem is that they just don't work that well if thinking is the goal.

Lastly, finding and using quality resources presents an ongoing challenge to Social Studies teachers. Textbooks are the most commonly used resource. This makes sense. Almost all classrooms have them, and they present information through efficient explanations, pictures, charts, and other visual methods. And teachers do not need to go looking for them, which may be the biggest benefit of all. Yet, textbooks contain a number of problems too: they usually present surface-level understandings; their reading level is often too high for students; and they always contain unaddressed bias. Further, and perhaps most important, they do a bad job of presenting multiple perspectives about issues and events. Teachers, then, need to find resources on their own that can offer students more depth and more varied perspectives. These other types of resources exist. Libraries and museums will often loan entire boxes of varied materials to teachers. Nonprofits and NGOs sometimes provide materials about specific topics. And the Internet, of course, is awash in historical information. The challenge for teachers is creating the time to acquire these resources and learning how to use them, especially when teachers are so often overwhelmed by the other responsibilities of their jobs.

Even with all of these challenges, quality teaching in Social Studies is crucial. Social Studies helps to create a public that is literate about social and historical issues, can analyze problems through context, and has a global awareness of the challenges facing society. To create such a public, students must be presented with meaningful problems and asked to engage in analytical thinking. Forty-five minutes a week of Social Studies won't cut it, nor will a reductionist focus on test scores or teaching methods that keep students disengaged. Teachers face significant challenges in teaching Social Studies. **But the urgency to confront those challenges in order to create this much needed public has never been greater.**

It's your turn. Take another look at the closing sentence in your essay. Make sure that it complements the opening sentence of your introduction. Also make sure that it gives readers the last impression that you want them to have about your essay.

STEP 9: WRITE COMPLETE SENTENCES

Now that you've written a draft of your essay, we need to start checking, editing, and revising it. We'll start with checking to make sure that you've written complete sentences. These are the three things that I want you to take away from this step:

1. Write complete sentences.
2. Use simple punctuation, focusing on using periods and commas correctly.
3. Put commas where you pause.

It's easy to not write complete sentences and to accidentally write fragments and run-ons. In fact, students often don't know whether or not they are writing fragments or run-ons, and that can cause real problems. Complete sentences express complete thoughts. Fragments are sentences that are incomplete, and run-ons are sentences that go on too long and contain too many ideas. We'll review how sentences are put together and how to fix mistakes. I also want you to only use simple punctuation. In fact, I'm going to suggest that you use only periods and commas. You don't need any other punctuation marks to write a great essay. It's too easy to make mistakes, and you don't benefit from complicated punctuation. Just be simple and direct. We're also going to review comma usage. I see students make mistakes all the time with commas, so I'm going to give you a simple rule you can use that will help you to avoid these common mistakes.

A Basic Review of Complete Sentences

Fragments – Incomplete Sentences

The difference between complete sentences and fragments is simple – but easy to miss. Remember that complete sentences express complete thoughts, while fragments express incomplete thoughts. Here are two examples:

Fragment: The new fence around the field.
Complete: The new fence around the field looks great.

The difference between the two is that the first has both a subject (fence) and a verb (looks). The second only has a subject (fence). But it's also more than this. Incomplete sentences are fragments. There are lots of ways that sentences can be incomplete. Sometimes it's the verb tense; sometimes a verb is lacking; sometimes it's an extra phrase. It's more helpful, I think, to gain an understanding of what a complete sentence *feels* like when you read it. This also means that fragments, or incomplete sentences, *feel* incomplete; they feel like something is missing. I'm going to give you a list of complete and incomplete sentences so that you can compare them:

Fragment: Problem-solving so that the student just sees questions and answers.
Complete: Problem-solving, so that the student just sees questions and answers, isn't that helpful.

Fragment: Which states that truth is difficult to find.
Complete: The book states that truth is difficult to find.

Fragment: Although small businesses increased their hiring last year.
Complete: Although small businesses increased their hiring last year, wages remain flat.

Fragment: The text found by many to be difficult.
Complete: The text was found by many to be difficult.

Fragment: Themes with widespread agreement within the scientific community.
Complete: There aren't that many themes with widespread agreement within the scientific community.

Fragment: Small businesses gaining ground among many competitors.
Complete: A few small businesses gained ground among many competitors.

Let's look more closely at two of these fragments to see why they are fragments. Here's the first one:

1. Which states that truth is difficult to find.

What states that truth is difficult to find? There is no subject to this sentence. It's the first "Which" that mainly makes this thought incomplete. We could change it to: "I read a book which states that truth is difficult to find." Now that is a complete thought. We could also simplify the phrase to "Truth is difficult to find." That is also a complete thought. However, if we just took off the first "Which" and have the sentence read – "States that truth is difficult to find," we'd still have an incomplete thought. Who states or what states that truth is difficult to find? Notice the feeling of incompleteness?

Here's another:

2. Although small businesses increased their hiring last year.

Example #2 is also an incomplete thought. Only one word makes it incomplete. Can you find it? It's the word "Although." "Although" tells us that something else is coming next, such as in "Although I wasn't hungry, I ate dessert anyway." The word "although," in this case, makes the phrase dependent on a different phrase to be a complete thought. In the case of small businesses, here's what it looks like in comparison:

Fragment: Although small businesses increased hiring last year.

Complete: Small businesses increased hiring last year.
or
Complete: Although small businesses increased hiring last year, wages remain flat.

Take off the "Although," and you now have a complete thought. Or add an independent clause, such as "wages remain flat," to make the thought complete.

Run-ons – Too Many Thoughts
Run-on sentences are the opposite problem of fragments. Whereas fragments feel incomplete, run-ons contain too many ideas and should be broken up into smaller complete sentences. Run-ons either have commas where a period should go (called a "comma splice"), or they just blend two sentences together without any

punctuation at all (called a "fused sentence"). I'll give you a series of run-ons and complete sentences to illustrate what I mean.

Run-on: It's very weird, I like solving problems, but when something is actually a problem to me I just wish I could solve it faster.

Complete: It's very weird. I like solving problems, but when something is actually a problem to me, I just wish I could solve it faster.

Run-on: That's only because it's me right now and how I feel but as for children in elementary school, sometimes they don't even know why they receive such a grade all they know is that it's bad and they will be in trouble with mom or dad for it.

Complete: That's only because it's me right now and how I feel. But as for children in elementary school, sometimes they don't even know why they receive such a grade. All they know is that it's bad, and they will be in trouble with mom or dad for it.

Run-on: I feel as though grading takes you off course with worries and sometimes teachers that do grade they never tell you as to why you received that grade, which leaves you feeling lost and also unaccomplished.

Complete: I feel as though grading takes you off course with worries. Sometimes teachers who do grade never tell you why you received that grade, which can leave you feeling lost and unaccomplished.

Run-on: So change is good, and most of the time it is for the better, the crazy thing is that these writers have been around for a while and we are still learning from them today.

Complete: So change is good, and most of the time it is for the better. The crazy thing is that these writers have been around for a while, and we are still learning from them today.

Let's look more closely at two of these run-ons and get a better sense of why they are run-ons. Here's the first one:

- It's very weird, I like solving problems, but when something is actually a problem to me I just wish I could solve it faster, because I think that is much more valuable to have a person than what most people know.

I count at least 4 thoughts in that sentence. I'll break them apart:

1. It's very weird.
2. I like solving problems.
3. But when something is actually a problem to me, I just wish I could solve it faster.
4. I think that is much more valuable to have a person than what most people know.

If I separated each thought by periods, it would look like this:

- It's very weird. I like solving problems. But when something is actually a problem to me, I just wish I could solve it faster. I think that is much more valuable to have a person than what most people know.

I don't know what that last sentence means, but I know it represents a complete thought (even if it still needs some work).

Let's look at the other run-on sentence:

- So change is good, and most of the time it is for the better, the crazy thing is that these writers have been around for a while and we are still learning from them today.

I count 4 thoughts again.

1. So change is good.
2. most of the time it is for the better.
3. the crazy thing is that these writers have been around for a while
4. we are still learning from them today.

These 4 thoughts should be grouped into two compound sentences. A compound sentence is a sentence that combines two complete (and related) thoughts, usually with a conjunction. It would look like this:

- So change is good, and most of the time it is for the better. The crazy thing is that these writers have been around for a while, and we are still learning from them today.

Three Types of Complete Sentences

There are three types of complete sentences: simple, compound, and complex. A simple sentence states only one complete thought. Compound and complex sentences join two thoughts together, but they do it in different ways. It's not necessary to remember the names of these types of complete sentences. But having a general understanding of the different forms complete sentences can take can help you to gain a better feeling for when sentences are complete or incomplete. Here are some examples:

Simple:	I turned in the folder I had been working on for the past eight weeks.

Compound:	I turned in the folder I had been working on for the past eight weeks, but I forgot to include two documents.

Complex:	I turned in the folder I had been working on for the past eight weeks, even though I didn't think it was very good.

The difference between a compound and a complex sentence is in the type of conjunction that each one uses. A compound sentence uses what is called a "coordinating conjunction," while a complex sentence uses what is called a "subordinating conjunction."

Coordinating Conjunctions = and, or, nor, for, yet, but, so

Subordinating Conjunctions = whenever, because, before, since, after, although, and other words like these

A Simple Rule for Using Commas

The other common mistake that students make is with commas. Commas seem simple, but they cause people a lot of problems. We either use too many of them or not enough of them. And they are easy to put in the wrong places. Teachers usually tell students all of the rules for where and when to use commas. But because so many people make so many mistakes using commas, it seems clear to me that just teaching those rules usually doesn't work. So, let me make this simpler for you. Instead of worrying about comma rules, do this instead: *Only put commas where you pause.* This means that when you read a sentence out loud, notice where you naturally pause and then insert a comma there. The chances are that you'll put the comma in the right place. Let's do some practice.

Read the following sentences out loud and put in any missing commas (cover the answers below):

1. The fan cheering loudest is my mother.
2. Lauren my cousin is visiting me.
3. Someone that I met at your party once lived in Ireland.
4. Adam a friend of mine from camp will be visiting me next week.
5. The man who won the lottery gave his money to charity.

Answer: The sentences numbered 2 and 4 need commas. In sentence #2, we pause after "Lauren" and after "cousin." So, the sentence should look like this: "Lauren, my cousin, is visiting me." In sentence #4, we pause after "Adam" and after "camp." The sentence should look like this: "Adam, a friend of mine from camp, will be visiting me next week." The other sentences don't need commas because we read straight through them.

Let's look at two more sentences that contain phrases. The first one needs commas, but the second one does not.

1. My neighbor, who is a little busybody, came around last night asking questions.
2. Teachers who use hands-on teaching methods tend to get better results with their students.

Each phrase starts with the word "who." Each phrase describes the subject of the sentence. In the first sentence, the phrase describes the neighbor. In the second sentence, it describes teachers. So why does the first phrase require commas but the second phrase does not? It's because the first phrase really has nothing to do with the sentence. It's just extra information that describes the neighbor. I could take it out and the sentence would not really be affected. But if I took out the phrase in the second sentence, it would change the meaning of the sentence. It's more important, so I don't set it off with commas.

Did you notice something else? In the first sentence, I pause right before and right after the phrase when I read it out loud. But I don't pause in the second sentence when I read it out loud. I just read it straight through. So, I can give you more examples of commas setting off dependent clauses, appositive phrases, lists of items, etc. But I'm not sure how useful that is. If you can simply find where the pause is when you read the sentence out loud, you'll find where to put the comma...and you'll put it in the right spot regardless of which punctuation rule you are looking at. Here are some more examples of how to mark pauses with commas:

- Grades are inferences, personal interpretations on the part of the teacher, not infallible truths about students' mastery.
- Surely, schooling has something to do with this conception.
- At its core, a disciplinary approach to history embraces interpretation and evidence-based reasoning.
- They can bribe the students by saying, "Only students with straight A's can be allowed at the pizza party.
- Differentiated instruction is a tool that students can lean on, to have as support when they are having trouble.

Another common problem with commas is that people often put commas before a verb, especially is the subject of the sentence is long. For example:
- The old movie theater around the corner, is my favorite.

You don't pause between "corner" and "is," so there is no need for a comma:
- The old movie theater around the corner is my favorite.

STEP 10: USE TRANSITIONS LIKE THEY ARE ROAD SIGNS

Students too often overlook transitions. This is a mistake. Transitions are not just essential components of your writing; they are fundamental to making your case. Transitions come in two basic types: in-paragraph transitions and between-paragraph transitions. These two types of transitions share the same basic function - they help guide your readers through your essay. Sure, you can and will use words such as first, second, next, and then, but if you want your essays to really be effective, you'll need to learn how to use transitions in a more sophisticated way.

In-Paragraph Transitions

You use transitions within paragraphs to distinguish one idea from another. You'll usually use simple words or phrases for this - what many people think of and call "transition words." Students often leave them out and just skip from one idea to the next. That makes an essay hard to read, though. Like a road sign tells a driver what is coming ahead on the road, a transition helps readers to understand the direction that an essay is taking. You probably know the common "transition words," such as however, next, therefore, thus, further, furthermore, additionally, and many others. The simple key to using them well is to decide what is happening in the next sentence and then pick the right word to express that coming action in relationship to the current idea.

In addition, you can also transition from one idea to the next within a paragraph by how you shape your sentences. These transitions don't rely on transition "words" to move the argument; instead, they use the shape of the narrative. Here's a sample paragraph that uses both types of transitions. I'll put them in italics:

> Defining quality in teaching is unusually difficult. Were anyone serious about this issue, they would soon realize that quality is an ineffable concept, as the best-selling book by Pirsig (1974) made clear. Defining quality always requires value judgments about which disagreements abound. Studying teaching cross-culturally makes this evident (Alexander, 2000). A high-quality teacher in India does not allow questioning by students. Students simply listen for hours on end. *The*

opposite is true in many American classes, where students are expected to raise questions during class. Alexander (2000) found that maintaining discipline is not part of any definition of quality in Russia or India because there are almost no discipline problems in their schools. *But in the organizationally complex world of American and British schools,* with individualization of some activities, promotion of collaboration and negotiation, and a concern for students' feelings, there is a greater incidence of behavior problems. *Thus,* American and British teachers of high quality must have classroom management skills that are unnecessary in Russia or India. (Berliner, 2005)

The author uses a transition word, "thus," in the last sentence. The word "thus" signals a conclusion to the present thought. But he still maneuvers around his topic arguing different points. He does this with his sentences. His use of "The opposite is true in many American classes" in line 6 shows a contrast. He doesn't need to write, "In contrast." The sentence takes care of that for him. In line 9, the author shows another contrast with "But in the organizationally complex world of American and British schools." Yes, the author does use the word "But" which signals a contrast. But he sets up the full contrast with the full introductory phrase to that sentence.

Here's a different paragraph that also effectively uses in-paragraph transitions. It leans on transition words, but the text still flows smoothly. Again, I'll italicize the transition words:

But what do we know about Socrates and the method he used to interrogate Athenians in the agora? *And what are we talking about* when we call it the "Socratic method?" *As it turns out,* we may be mistaking common phrasing for common practice. *After all,* classrooms in which the Socratic method is ostensibly employed are hardly all the same. Teachers are at the center of some and at the periphery of others. Talk is common in all, but it includes chaotic zigzagging in one class and linear directionality in another. Socratic classrooms can be relaxed or tense, loud or quiet, large or small. They can, *in other words,* seem as different from each other as they seem from classes in which other methods are the basis of instruction. (Schneider, 2012)

These are the major transition words/phrases the author uses:

- **"But what do we know"** = signals a contrast
- **"And what are we talking about"** = signals a question
- **"As it turns out"** = in actuality
- **"After all"** = as we all know
- **"in other words"** = signals a conclusion, but also a restatement

Take a look at what the paragraph would look like without those transition words:

> Socrates used a method to interrogate Athenians in the agora. We call it the "Socratic method." We may be mistaking common phrasing for common practice. Classrooms in which the Socratic method is ostensibly employed are hardly all the same. Teachers are at the center of some and at the periphery of others. Talk is common in all, but it includes chaotic zigzagging in one class and linear directionality in another. Socratic classrooms can be relaxed or tense, loud or quiet, large or small. They can seem as different from each other as they seem from classes in which other methods are the basis of instruction.

This revised paragraph doesn't have nearly the same meaning or effect as the original paragraph. That is what transitions do for you. They help to give your writing more meaning - and especially more precise meaning.

Let's examine one paragraph from our sample essay for how I use *In-Paragraph* transitions. I'll italicize all of the words and phrases used as transitions:

> *When Social Studies is tested,* teachers face a different problem: too much to teach in the time they have. *This often* leads teachers to engage in "inch deep and mile wide" teaching practices. *Compounding this time problem* is the fact that students usually come to Social Studies with little to no familiarity with the content. *Teachers then* spend considerable time on repetitive, "drill and kill" teaching practices in the hope they will help students to retain information at least until testing day. While many teachers would like to engage students in more meaningful activities, they

often do not feel they have time for it. *According to one high school history teacher* in a study by Kenneth Vogler (2005),

> I use the entire academic year preparing my students for the United States history subject exam. My choice of instructional delivery and materials is completely dependent on preparation for this test. Therefore, I do not use current events, long-term projects, or creative group/corporate work because this is not tested and the delivery format is not used. All my tests reflect the testing format of the subject area tests – multiple-choice and open ended questions (p. 19).

Some researchers claim that mandated accountability exams lead to a "just the facts, ma'am" approach to teaching social studies (Vogler & Virtue, 2007). *Other* researchers go further and contend that "because multiple-choice testing leads to multiple-choice teaching, the methods that teachers have in their arsenal become reduced, and teaching work is deskilled" (Smith, 1991, p. 10).

You'll notice that many of the first words in the sentences work as transitions. I do this because I want to smoothly guide my readers through my argument. You should try to do this too. But also notice that I don't write "The first point I'm going to make is…." Those kinds of transitions work, but they don't sound good.

Between-Paragraph Transitions

The other place to use transitions is when you are moving from one paragraph to the next. Sometimes you will use a transition word, but more likely you should use the sentences themselves as transitions. Let's examine our example essay. The italicized sentences are the transition sentences; these will be the first sentence in each paragraph. These sentences link ideas from paragraph to paragraph, helping to smooth the way for the idea in the next paragraph. They don't need to directly address the content of the last sentence of the preceding paragraph (although that is sometimes a good idea). Instead, they need to highlight a change in idea, from something previously discussed to what is coming next. We'll examine each one. I'm also going to italicize all of the *in-paragraph transitions*, just so you can see how they all work together to move readers smoothly through an argument:

> Teaching social studies is hard. Teachers face a variety of obstacles that can make their job feel impossible. Standardized testing creates significant pressure on teachers. State and school district

curriculum plans often ask too much of teachers and students: teach and learn too much content in too short of a time frame. This lack of time can pressure teachers to teach just facts. Sometimes social studies isn't tested, so it gets ignored for tested subjects that "matter." *Yet*, even when Social Studies is tested, those scores do not always fully count towards a school's accountability rating. Models of quality teaching can *also* be in short supply in Social Studies. *Further*, teachers often face a lack of resources to meaningfully teach Social Studies.

Teachers constantly struggle with a lack of time to teach. Standardized testing plays a crucial role in this time problem. When Social Studies is not tested, it tends to get ignored. Elementary schools routinely allot as little as 45 minutes a week to Social Studies. What meaningful teaching and learning can happen in only 45 minutes a week? Middle and high schools allow more scheduled time, but frequently subtract from that time by scheduling things such as pep rallies, school assemblies, and fundraising meetings during Social Studies classes. These practices send a clear picture to students that Social Studies, when it is not tested, is less important to the school than tested subjects.

When Social Studies is tested, teachers face a different problem: too much to teach in the time they have. This often leads teachers to engage in "inch deep and mile wide" teaching practices. *Compounding this time problem* is the fact that students usually come to Social Studies with little to no familiarity with the content. *Teachers then* spend considerable time on repetitive, "drill and kill" teaching practices in the hope they will help students to retain information at least until testing day. While many teachers would like to engage students in more meaningful activities, they often do not feel they have time for it. *According to one high school history teacher* in a study by Kenneth Vogler (2005),

> I use the entire academic year preparing my students for the United States history subject exam. My choice of instructional delivery and materials is completely dependent on preparation for this test. Therefore, I do not use current events, long-term projects, or creative group/corporate work because this is not tested and the delivery format is not used. All my tests reflect the testing format of the subject area tests – multiple-choice and open ended questions (p. 19).

Some researchers claim that mandated accountability exams lead to a "just the facts, ma'am" approach to teaching social studies (Vogler & Virtue,

2007). *Other* researchers go further and contend that "because multiple-choice testing leads to multiple-choice teaching, the methods that teachers have in their arsenal become reduced, and teaching work is deskilled" (Smith, 1991, p. 10).

Another reason Social Studies is hard to teach is that teachers have so few models of good Social Studies teaching. Most Social Studies teaching takes the form of "telling," in which teachers lecture, i.e. "tell" students information, perhaps show a picture or video, and then test students on the content. *In this paradigm,* students are not asked to actively learn, only to passively retain information. *There is a simple reason for this:* teachers usually teach the way they were taught when they were students. High schools and universities are notorious for this kind of passive teaching and learning. *So,* it makes sense that teachers continue to use these methods. The problem is that they just don't work that well if thinking is the goal.

Lastly, finding and using quality resources presents an ongoing challenge to Social Studies teachers. Textbooks are the most commonly used resource. This makes sense. Almost all classrooms have them, and they present information through efficient explanations, pictures, charts, and other visual methods. And teachers do not need to go looking for them, which may be the biggest benefit of all. *Yet,* textbooks contain a number of problems too: they usually present surface-level understandings; their reading level is often too high for students; and they always contain unaddressed bias. *Further,* and perhaps most important, they do a bad job of presenting multiple perspectives about issues and events. Teachers, *then,* need to find resources on their own that can offer students more depth and more varied perspectives. These other types of resources exist. Libraries and museums will often loan entire boxes of varied materials to teachers. Nonprofits and NGOs sometimes provide materials about specific topics. And the Internet, *of course,* is awash in historical information. The challenge for teachers is creating the time to acquire these resources and learning how to use them, especially when teachers are so often overwhelmed by the other responsibilities of their jobs.

Even with all of these challenges, quality teaching in Social Studies is crucial. Social Studies helps to create a public that is literate about social and historical issues, can analyze problems through context, and has a global awareness of the challenges facing society. *To create such a public,* students must be presented with meaningful problems and asked to engage in analytical thinking. Forty-five minutes a week of Social

Studies won't cut it, nor will a reductionist focus on test scores or teaching methods that keep students disengaged. Teachers face significant challenges in teaching Social Studies. But the urgency to confront those challenges in order to create this much needed public has never been greater.

Let's examine each of the above italicized sentences in turn.

1. *Teachers constantly struggle with a lack of time to teach:* The introduction mentions that teachers lack time to teach concepts in depth. I begin the second paragraph by jumping straight into this point. The first highlighted sentence, therefore, connects to one of the points made in the introduction and establishes the new topic for the paragraph.

2. *When Social Studies is tested, teachers face a different problem: too much to teach in the time they have:* The second highlighted sentence adds a new idea. I had been stating that social studies test scores don't count towards an accountability rating, so people cared less about it. In this sentence, I change this thought by claiming that "Even if social studies test scores do count…" I'm stating that, yes, social studies test scores usually don't count, but *even if they did count*, social studies teachers would still face daunting challenges.

3. *Another reason Social Studies is hard to teach is that teachers have so few models of good Social Studies teaching:* The third highlighted sentence adds to the list of reasons why teaching social studies is hard. It does this by stating that "another reason teaching Social Studies is hard…."

4. *Lastly, finding and using quality resources presents an ongoing challenge to Social Studies teachers:* The fourth highlighted sentence uses a typical transition word, "Lastly." This word signals to readers that that paragraph discusses the last item on the list of reasons why teaching Social Studies is hard.

5. *Even with all of these challenges, quality teaching in Social Studies is crucial:* The fifth highlighted sentence, which is in the conclusion, does two things. First, it recognizes all of the challenges that were previously discussed ("Even with all of these challenges"). Second, it puts this list of challenges into a new context (that "quality teaching in Social Studies is crucial").

Now it's your turn. Look through your essay and make sure you are using smooth transitions, both between paragraphs and within paragraphs. Use the information in this step to guide you. You want to make the experience of reading your essay as smooth and easy as possible. Decide where you need to blend ideas together and where you need to just jump/move to the next idea. However you do it, the ideas need to easily flow from one to the next.

STEP 11: PAY ATTENTION TO VERBS

In many ways, verbs are more important to your writing than are nouns and adjectives. Using the right verbs can add movement, color, and character to your writing. But bad verb choice can really hurt your writing. Selecting the wrong verbs can slow down your writing, making it feel clunky and ponderous to read. Also, mistakes with verbs just jump off of the page. So, it's crucial that you pay attention to the verbs you use. There are three things I want you to take away from this step:

1. Make subjects and verbs agree
2. Strengthen your verbs
3. Write in active voice

Make Subjects and Verbs Agree

One mistake that I often see is when subjects and verbs do not agree. I see it in students' papers, and I also see it in newspapers and other professional publications. These mistakes are easy to fix…if we know what to look for. Let's do a short review about subject/verb agreement. All sentences have subjects and predicates. Put simply, the subject is what the sentence is about and the predicate is what happens within the sentence. Here's a simple example:

> The girl hit the ball.

The subject is "The girl." The predicate is "hit the ball." The sentence is about the girl and hitting the ball is what happens in the sentence. We can divide the sentence like this:

> The girl / hit the ball.

We can break the sentence down into smaller component pieces: simple subject and simple predicate. The simple subject is usually one word, usually a noun or a pronoun, that the sentence is about, in this case "girl." The simple predicate is usually one word, a verb, that does the action, in this case "hit." Such a division looks like this:

girl / hit

The tense of these words must match. They should either both be singular or both be plural. These are three points about subject/verb agreement that you need to remember:

1. Simple subject = usually one word that the sentence is about
2. Simple predicate = usually one word (a verb) that does the action
3. These must match (either both be singular or both be plural)

Mistakes are easy to spot in shorter sentences, but they can be harder to spot in longer sentences, especially if the simple subject and simple predicate are far apart, such as in the sentence below:

- <u>Incorrect</u>: The right **toe** of her custom-made bowling shoes **are** worn through from her follow-through.
- <u>Correct</u>: The right **toe** of her custom-made bowling shoes **is** worn through from her follow-through.

In the examples above, "toe" is the simple subject. Since the simple subject is singular, the simple predicate must also be singular. That's why "are" is incorrect and "is" is correct.

Here are a few more examples:

- **One** of the benefits **is** that it meets the needs of diverse learners.
- The **elephants** in the circus that just came to town **are** well trained.
- That **man** with the crooked nose who looks a lot like my uncle Phil **has been staring** at us this entire time.
- This **recipe** for brownies that has been passed down for generations **calls** for nutmeg.

- **Allegations** by a previously unknown student **were** to expose a scandal.

[Practice 11.1.] Take a moment and practice. Mark the correct verb. The answers are listed at the end of this step:

1. The lines in that old historic post office (was/were) crowded.
2. One of the statues that has been touring a lot of museums (is/are) beautiful.
3. The past three leaders of the campus debate society (has/have) all been men.
4. The tomatoes in the garden in the backyard (is/are) particularly sweet.
5. The safety record of all the workers in all of the company factories (is/are) superb.

If the subject comes *after* the verb, we just look backwards. Find what the sentence is about and match that tense to the verb. In the examples below, I **bold** the simple subjects and predicates:

1. There **are** more **matches** on the shelf.
2. Here **come** the **lions**.
3. How many times **has she** filled her plate?

If two or more words are in the subject, look at the type of conjunction that joins those words. You'll need to determine how the items are used to know whether or not they are singular or plural. Here are three examples:
1. A tack or a nail was used to put up the poster. (Singular – refers to the nail or tack, each as just one thing)
2. Football and soccer are interesting games. (Plural – refers to football and soccer as two different things combined)
3. Bacon and eggs is my favorite breakfast. (Singular – refers to bacon and eggs as making up one thing)

Take another moment and do a little more practice. The answers to both practice sets (11.1 and 11.2) are listed at the end of this step:

[Practice 11.2]

1. Which records (has/have) Marsha brought with her?
2. Here (is/are) the stamps from Sweden.
3. There (was/were) three ducks on the pond out back.
4. Coconut pie and apple cake (was/were) our choices.
5. Either Sam or Elsa (drives/drive) the car.
6. Peanut butter and jelly (is/are) my favorite sandwich.

Strengthen Your Verbs

Another way to polish your writing is to strengthen your verbs. Why run when you can sprint? Why talk softly when you can whisper? Why have a large impact when you can propel? Forget adverbs. They usually only serve to slow down writing. You want verbs that illustrate action. Let's look at some examples:

Weaker: Watson's work strongly impacted the field of physics.
Stronger: Watson's work propelled the field of physics forward.

Weaker: Our group looked carefully at the data.
Stronger: Our group scrutinized the data.

Weaker: Students were talking about the main idea of the story.
Stronger: Students discussed the main idea of the story.

Weaker: These new ideas traveled quickly around the world.
Stronger: These new ideas rocketed around the world.

Weaker: The students slowly walked into the quiet classroom.
Stronger: The students crept into the quiet classroom.

Weaker: The wild horses ran quickly across the mountain pasture.
Stronger: The wild horses sprinted across the mountain pasture.

Weaker: The architect thought hard about how to overcome the problem.
Stronger: The architect pondered how to overcome the problem.

Weaker: Eagles flew above the trees.
Stronger: Eagles soared above the trees.

You don't want to fill your essay with this kind of language. But where appropriate, it can add spark and color to your writing.

Write in Active Voice

Good writing tends to be active, not passive. Active voice propels writing forward, while passive voice can slow it down. I'm talking about using active instead of passive verbs. A simple way to remember the difference between active and passive voice is that active voice does something, while passive voice has something done to it. Here are some examples:

Passive: We were confused during the activity.
Active: We did not understand the activity.
Passive: Updike is commonly considered by critics to be a model of a great writer.
Active: Critics call Updike a great writer.

Passive: We were late getting home.
Active: We arrived home late.

Passive: Now we have a paragraph that is focused and that makes a clear point.
Active: Now we have a focused paragraph that makes a clear point.

Here's a simple rule: if you use linking or helping verbs, then you are writing in passive voice. To reduce passive voice, watch out for using too many of these verbs:

am   is   are   was   were   be   being   been

Let's edit a short passage for passive voice:

> Sometimes children **are embarrassed** for the reason that they **were singled out** previously which leads to tuning out or refusing to speak out in front of peers which **is why** cooperative learning **is a positive and essential thing**. Not only **is cooperative learning helpful** for children but it boosts their self-esteem and interpersonal relations. Conducting research has only proven that cooperating and interacting with peers has proven to **be effective** and I **am for** this method.

I put the passive verbs in the above paragraph in **bold**. Take this phrase: "children are embarrassed." This is passive. Active would be "children *feel* embarrassed." I'll go through the passage and edit it for passive-to-active voice, as well as make the writing more efficient:

> Singling out children in the classroom can cause them to feel embarrassed and withdraw from a lesson. Cooperative learning can counteract these effects. It can generate greater engagement in the classroom, boost students' self-esteem, and develop their interpersonal relations.

Notice how smoothly the revised passage reads compared to the original. It's much less wordy, more active, and makes a greater impact. And it's more efficient, which makes it more pleasant to read.

We'll do one more:

> There **was** a study conducted using economically disadvantaged Hispanic participants focusing on social studies at the elementary level in a cooperative learning group versus children who received instruction using a traditional approach. The 12-week study **was** conducted in two elementary schools in eight classrooms using Johnson and Johnson "Brown Book" workshops. There **was** a pre-test administered in the beginning and a post-test at the end. All teachers used the same content but different ways of instructing it to their students.

Now I'll revise it:

> Researchers conducted a twelve-week study on cooperative learning with economically disadvantaged Hispanic students. The study focused on social studies at the elementary level. In this quasi-experimental study,

one group of classrooms used traditional instruction, and the other group used cooperative learning strategies. Both groups used Johnson and Johnson "Brown Book" workshops. Researchers gave students a pre-test in the beginning of the unit and a post-test at the end.

The revised passage is only a little shorter than the original. But it has more emphasis and movement. It reads more efficiently and makes a clearer point. One simple way to check yourself for too much passive voice is to watch for those verbs: am, is, are, was, were, be, being, been. If you find yourself using them too often, go back, take them out, and replace them with more active verbs.

Apply This to Our Sample Essay

Let's apply this information to our sample essay. I'll copy our essay again below and **BOLD** two sentences that we can change:

Teaching social studies is hard. Teachers face a variety of obstacles that can make their job feel impossible. Standardized testing creates significant pressure on teachers. State and school district curriculum plans often ask too much of teachers and students: teach and learn too much content in too short of a time frame. This lack of time can pressure teachers to teach just facts. Sometimes social studies isn't tested, so it gets ignored for tested subjects that "matter." Yet, even when Social Studies is tested, those scores do not always fully count towards a school's accountability rating. Models of quality teaching can also be in short supply in Social Studies. Further, teachers often face a lack of resources to meaningfully teach Social Studies.

Teachers constantly struggle with a lack of time to teach. Standardized testing plays a crucial role in this time problem. When Social Studies is not tested, it tends to get ignored. Elementary schools routinely allot as little as 45 minutes a week to Social Studies. What meaningful teaching and learning can happen in only 45 minutes a week? Middle and high schools allow more scheduled time, but frequently subtract from that time by scheduling things such as pep rallies, school assemblies, and fundraising meetings during Social Studies classes. These practices send a clear picture to students that Social Studies, when it is not tested, is less important to the school than tested subjects.

When Social Studies is tested, teachers face a different problem: too much to teach in the time they have. This often leads teachers to engage in "inch deep and mile wide" teaching practices. Compounding this time problem is the fact that students usually come to Social Studies with little to no familiarity with the content. Teachers then spend considerable time on repetitive, "drill and kill" teaching practices in the hope they will help students to retain information at least until testing day. While many teachers would like to engage students in more meaningful activities, they often do not feel they have time for it. According to one high school history teacher in a study by Kenneth Vogler (2005),

> I use the entire academic year preparing my students for the United States history subject exam. My choice of instructional delivery and materials is completely dependent on preparation for this test. Therefore, I do not use current events, long-term projects, or creative group/corporate work because this is not tested and the delivery format is not used. All my tests reflect the testing format of the subject area tests – multiple-choice and open ended questions (p. 19).

Some researchers claim that mandated accountability exams lead to a "just the facts, ma'am" approach to teaching social studies (Vogler & Virtue, 2007). Other researchers go further and contend that "because multiple-choice testing leads to multiple-choice teaching, the methods that teachers have in their arsenal become reduced, and teaching work is deskilled" (Smith, 1991, p. 10).

Another reason Social Studies is hard to teach is that teachers have so few models of good Social Studies teaching. Most Social Studies teaching takes the form of "telling," in which teachers lecture, i.e. "tell" students information, perhaps show a picture or video, and then test students on the content. In this paradigm, students are not asked to actively learn, only to passively retain information. **There is a simple reason for this: teachers usually teach the way they were taught when they were students.** High schools and universities are notorious for this kind of passive teaching and learning. So, it makes sense that teachers continue to use these methods. The problem is that they just don't work that well if thinking is the goal.

Lastly, finding and using quality resources presents an ongoing challenge to Social Studies teachers. Textbooks are the most commonly used resource. This makes sense. Almost all classrooms have them, and they present information through efficient explanations, pictures, charts, and other visual methods. And teachers do not need to go looking for them, which may be the biggest benefit of all. Yet, textbooks contain a number of problems too: they usually present surface-level understandings; their reading level is often too high for students; and they always contain unaddressed bias. Further, and perhaps most important, they do a bad job of presenting multiple perspectives about issues and events. Teachers, then, need to find resources on their own that can offer students more depth and more varied perspectives. These other types of resources exist. Libraries and museums will often loan entire boxes of varied materials to teachers. Nonprofits and NGOs sometimes provide materials about specific topics. And the Internet, of course, is awash in historical information. The challenge for teachers is creating the time to acquire these resources and learning how to use them, especially when teachers are so often overwhelmed by the other responsibilities of their jobs.

Even with all of these challenges, quality teaching in Social Studies is crucial. **Social Studies helps to create a public that is literate about social and historical issues, can analyze problems through context, and has a global awareness of the challenges facing society.** To create such a public, students must be presented with meaningful problems and asked to engage in analytical thinking. Forty-five minutes a week of Social Studies won't cut it, nor will a reductionist focus on test scores or teaching methods that keep students disengaged. Teachers face significant challenges in teaching Social Studies. But the urgency to confront those challenges in order to create this much needed public has never been greater.

The two sentences in bold can be changed to a more active voice. Here's the first sentence. I'm going to take out the "is:"

> Original: There is a simple reason for this: teachers usually teach the way they were taught when they were students.
> More active: A simple reason explains this: teachers usually teach the way their teachers taught them.

Now for the second sentence. This involves a more complicated change, even though I'm still only trying to delete the "is:"

Original: Social Studies helps to create a public that is literate about social and historical issues, can analyze problems through context, and has a global awareness of the challenges facing society.
More active: Social studies helps to create a literate public that cares about social and historical issues, that can analyze problems through context, and that has a global awareness of the challenges facing society.

Now I'll insert these two more active sentences back into our essay:

Teaching social studies is hard. Teachers face a variety of obstacles that can make their job feel impossible. Standardized testing creates significant pressure on teachers. State and school district curriculum plans often ask too much of teachers and students: teach and learn too much content in too short of a time frame. This lack of time can pressure teachers to teach just facts. Sometimes social studies isn't tested, so it gets ignored for tested subjects that "matter." Yet, even when Social Studies is tested, those scores do not always fully count towards a school's accountability rating. Models of quality teaching can also be in short supply in Social Studies. Further, teachers often face a lack of resources to meaningfully teach Social Studies.

Teachers constantly struggle with a lack of time to teach. Standardized testing plays a crucial role in this time problem. When Social Studies is not tested, it tends to get ignored. Elementary schools routinely allot as little as 45 minutes a week to Social Studies. What meaningful teaching and learning can happen in only 45 minutes a week? Middle and high schools allow more scheduled time, but frequently subtract from that time by scheduling things such as pep rallies, school assemblies, and fundraising meetings during Social Studies classes. These practices send a clear picture to students that Social Studies, when it is not tested, is less important to the school than tested subjects.

When Social Studies is tested, teachers face a different problem: too much to teach in the time they have. This often leads teachers to engage in "inch deep and mile wide" teaching practices. Compounding this time problem is the fact that students usually come to Social Studies with little to no familiarity with the content. Teachers then spend considerable time on repetitive, "drill and kill" teaching practices in the hope they will help students to retain information at least until testing day. While many teachers would like to engage students in more meaningful activities, they often do not feel they have time for it. According to one high school history teacher in a study by Kenneth Vogler (2005),

> I use the entire academic year preparing my students for the United States history subject exam. My choice of instructional delivery and materials is completely dependent on preparation for this test. Therefore, I do not use current events, long-term projects, or creative group/corporate work because this is not tested and the delivery format is not used. All my tests reflect the testing format of the subject area tests – multiple-choice and open ended questions (p. 19).

Some researchers claim that mandated accountability exams lead to a "just the facts, ma'am" approach to teaching social studies (Vogler & Virtue, 2007). Other researchers go further and contend that "because multiple-choice testing leads to multiple-choice teaching, the methods that teachers have in their arsenal become reduced, and teaching work is deskilled" (Smith, 1991, p. 10).

Another reason Social Studies is hard to teach is that teachers have so few models of good Social Studies teaching. Most Social Studies teaching takes the form of "telling," in which teachers lecture, i.e. "tell" students information, perhaps show a picture or video, and then test students on the content. In this paradigm, students are not asked to actively learn, only to passively retain information. **A simple reason explains this: teachers usually teach the way their teachers taught them.** High schools and universities are notorious for this kind of passive teaching and learning. So, it makes sense that teachers continue to use these methods. The problem is that they just don't work that well if thinking is the goal.

Lastly, finding and using quality resources presents an ongoing challenge to Social Studies teachers. Textbooks are the most commonly used resource. This makes sense. Almost all classrooms have them, and they present information through efficient explanations, pictures, charts, and other visual methods. And teachers do not need to go looking for them, which may be the biggest benefit of all. Yet, textbooks contain a number of problems too: they usually present surface-level understandings; their reading level is often too high for students; and they always contain unaddressed bias. Further, and perhaps most important, they do a bad job of presenting multiple perspectives about issues and events. Teachers, then, need to find resources on their own that can offer students more depth and more varied perspectives. These other types of resources exist. Libraries and museums will often loan entire boxes of varied materials to teachers. Nonprofits and NGOs sometimes provide materials about specific topics. And the Internet, of course, is awash in historical information. The challenge for teachers is creating the time to acquire these resources and learning how to use them, especially when teachers are so often overwhelmed by the other responsibilities of their jobs.

Even with all of these challenges, quality teaching in Social Studies is crucial. **Social studies helps to create a literate public that cares about social and historical issues, that can analyze problems through context, and that has a global awareness of the challenges facing society.** To create such a public, students must be presented with meaningful problems and asked to engage in analytical thinking. Forty-five minutes a week of Social Studies won't cut it, nor will a reductionist focus on test scores or teaching methods that keep students disengaged. Teachers face significant challenges in teaching Social Studies. But the urgency to confront those challenges in order to create this much needed public has never been greater.

[Practice 11.1 answers]
1. The lines in that old historic post office were crowded.
2. One of the statues that has been touring a lot of museums is beautiful.
3. The past three leaders of the campus debate society have all been men.
4. The tomatoes in the garden in the backyard are particularly sweet.
5. The safety record of all the workers in all of the company factories is superb.

[Practice 11.2 answers]
1. Which records has Marsha brought with her?
2. Here are the stamps from Sweden.
3. There were three ducks on the pond out back.
4. Coconut pie and apple cake were our choices.
5. Either Sam or Elsa drives the car.
6. Peanut butter and jelly is my favorite sandwich.

STEP 12: POLISH YOUR WRITING

The last editing step is to polish your writing. You have an introduction and a conclusion that works. You've created a strong argument. You've guided your readers through that argument with clear and easy to follow transitions. You've crafted solid sentences and paragraphs. Now we need to just make sure that the last crucial details within our writing are nicely honed. This step will focus on 3 common problems that people make in their essays. At the end of this step, we're going to apply some of these points to our sample essay:

1. Eliminate wordy sentences and paragraphs
2. Keep your writing parallel
3. Don't write "I believe" or "I think"

Eliminate Wordy Sentences and Paragraphs

It's usually a problem if your writing is too short. That indicates that you haven't put enough depth into your analysis. But it's also a problem if your writing is too wordy. Wordy writing is not fun to read. Worse, it takes up space that could be used for better, richer analysis. There are many ways to reduce wordiness, so we'll look at a few. We'll start with sentences and then move to paragraphs. Read the following sentence:

- Considering students' success as a priority, we must prepare with the best strategies to teach them social studies in an enrichment environment where students can feel comfortable to learn.

The key to reducing wordiness is writing simply and directly. Each word should have a specific purpose: just get to the point and use as few words as possible to make your point. The above sentence uses too many words to make its point. We don't need to refer to students three times (students', them, and students). I'm not sure we need the words "considering" or "enrichment." Those words should be implied. Here's a revised version:

- We must teach Social Studies in a comfortable and engaging environment, with student success as our priority.

Here are a few more examples of wordy sentences and ways to revise them:

Wordy: Students can do so much to help society and to make the world a better place, but if society did not place any value on education then there would be a lot less students interested.

Revised: Society must value education in order to draw out students' potential to impact the world.

Wordy: Today's teachers have much to take into consideration in order to educate all students equally regardless of the students' background in order to effectively teach today's culturally diverse classroom and ensure student success in comprehension in content areas.

Revised: Teachers today have much to consider to ensure students' success in learning content, as well as to facilitate culturally diverse classrooms.

Now let's take a look at wordy paragraphs. Let's start with this one:

- Students are being put in classrooms and basically drilled for state assessments and not allowed to enjoy learning and get them motivated to learn any kind of subject. I can say that in my own experience as a mother, I see my 6th grader and she tells me that she loves learning everyday but that the learning is not as fun as before.

Let's try to shorten this. I'll do it in steps. For the first sentence, we can assume that students are in classrooms. Where else would they be in a school? You don't need "basically." Just write: "Students are being drilled for state assessments". Are students really not allowed to enjoy learning? Is that against the rules? Or does it just feel that way? And are students actually kept from learning subject matter? Let's phrase the first sentence like this:

- Students spend too much time being drilled for state assessments, which can hurt their love for learning.

For the second sentence, don't write "I can say that in my own experience." There's no need to write "I can say." You're already doing that just by writing. Nor do you need "own." It's redundant. Also, you really don't need to identify yourself as a mother; referencing your "6th grader" will do that for you. Also, why write "I see my 6th grader and she tells me?" Just write, "My 6th grader tells me." And if she loves learning every day, then she loves learning, so we can leave that part out as well. So, let's see what we have so far:

- In my experience, my 6th grader tells me that she loves learning, but not as much now as before.

When we put them together, we get this. Do you see how much cleaner, clearer, and faster these sentences are than the original?:

- Students spend too much time being drilled for state assessments, which can hurt their love for learning. In my experience, my 6th grader tells me that she loves learning, but not as much now as before.

We'll do one more. Check out this paragraph:

- Are you someone who learns cooperatively or alone? As I was once told, "learning is social." Most students learn from each other. Cooperative learning is a method of instruction that has students working together in groups, usually with the goal of completing a specific task. Using cooperative learning among social studies will help students learn more than traditional teaching. Conducting research has proven that cooperative learning is an outstanding method to use in the classroom. Therefore, as you read you too will be convinced.

The first three sentences do little to help establish to the topic. They seem to just be extra to try to connect with readers. Eliminate them. The fourth through sixth sentences advance the topic. But the last sentence doesn't work. So, we're down to this:

- Cooperative learning is a method of instruction that has students working together in groups, usually with the goal of completing a specific task. Using cooperative learning among social studies will help students learn more than traditional teaching. Conducting research has proven that cooperative learning is an outstanding method to use in the classroom.

Let me edit it a bit more. I'm going to change the order of the second and third sentences. The only sentence I need to change is the second (now third) sentence. I don't know what "Conducting research has proven" means. Just write "Research shows that." It's much clearer and to the point. Here's the revised version:

- Cooperative learning is a method of instruction that has students working together in groups, usually with the goal of completing a specific task. Research shows that cooperative learning is an outstanding method to use in the classroom. Using cooperative learning with social studies will help students learn more than traditional teaching.

Now we have a focused paragraph that makes a clear point.

Keep Your Writing Parallel

Parallel writing means keeping things the same throughout a sentence. It means that nouns, adjectives, adverbs, and verbs must be in the same form. We're going to focus on parallel verbs and parallel lists. Here's a sentence that uses parallel verb tenses:

- Teachers may spend an enormous amount of time design**ing** assessments, provid**ing** feedback, and document**ing** students' progress.

All of the verb tenses are the same; here they all end in "ing" (it's called "present progressive").

The following sentence would *not* be parallel:

- Teachers **design** assessment, **provide** feedback, and **are documenting** students' progress.

This first two verbs are in present tense and last verb is in present progressive tense. They all need to be the same. The sentence should look like this:

- Teachers **design** assessment, **provide** feedback, and **document** students' progress.

Here's another sentence that is not parallel. I'll put the problem in bold:
- Verb tenses match; singular and plural align; and subjects **need to correspond** to verbs.

If the sentence was parallel it would read like this:
- Verb tenses match; singular and plural align; and subjects **correspond** to verbs.

Parallelism also applies to lists that don't include verbs. Here's an example of a problem:
- The film lacked a clear narrative, logical transitions, and the dialogue was unbelievable.

The problem is with the last item in the list. The last item isn't really an item; it's a new sentence. Here's a parallel version:
- The film lacked a clear narrative, logical transitions, and believable dialogue.

The sentence lists three things: clear narrative, logical transitions, and believable dialogue. You would need to keep those three items in the same format.

Here are two more sentences that have lists which are not parallel. I'll put the problems and solutions in bold. The first sentence uses a list of simple adjectives...or at least it begins that way:

Not parallel: The concert was loud, colorful, and **many people attended**.
Parallel: The concert was loud, colorful, and **crowded**.

The list is "loud, colorful," and then changes to "many people attended." It should just be "crowded."

This next sentence only has two items in the list. Both should use verbs that end in "ing:"

> Not parallel: **Taking** care of the elderly and **the education of children** are important to our plan.
> Parallel: **Taking** care of the elderly and **educating** children are important to our plan.

Below are a few more examples of incorrect/correct parallel structure:

> Not parallel: Moving deadlines, rephrasing questions, and **a change in techniques** are all ways of scaffolding students' success in the classroom.
> Parallel: Moving deadlines, rephrasing questions, and **changing techniques** are all ways of scaffolding students' success in the classroom.

> Not parallel: The school briefly banned those games, disturbed by the players' violence and **the fans behaving badly.**
> Parallel: The school briefly banned those games, disturbed by the players' violence and **the fans' behavior.**

> Not parallel: Early games, however, remained violent and **boredom.**
> Parallel: Early games, however, remained violent and **boring.**

Don't Write "I believe" or "I think"

It's not uncommon for students to write "I believe" or "I think" in their essays. This isn't necessary, and it slows down the writing. Of course you believe and/or think that. How do I know? Because you wrote it. Here are some examples:

> From: This I believe is the most effective.
> To: This is the most effective.

> From: I believe that after time has passed, history will vindicate that judgment.
> To: History will vindicate that judgment.

<u>From</u>: I believe, based on my own experience, that outlines are effective tools to help students to organize any piece of writing.
<u>To</u>: My experience indicates that outlines are effective tools for improving writing.

<u>From</u>: For me, I believe that progressivism promotes a child's environment and allows for questioning.
<u>To</u>: Progressivism promotes a child's environment and allows for questioning.

Apply This to Our Sample Essay

Let's now apply these points to our sample essay:

Teaching social studies is hard. Teachers face a variety of obstacles that can make their job feel impossible. Standardized testing creates significant pressure on teachers. State and school district curriculum plans often ask too much of teachers and students: teach and learn too much content in too short of a time frame. This lack of time can pressure teachers to teach just facts. Sometimes social studies isn't tested, so it gets ignored for tested subjects that "matter." Yet, even when Social Studies is tested, those scores do not always fully count towards a school's accountability rating. Models of quality teaching can also be in short supply in Social Studies. Further, teachers often face a lack of resources to meaningfully teach Social Studies.

Teachers constantly struggle with a lack of time to teach. Standardized testing plays a crucial role in this time problem. When Social Studies is not tested, it tends to get ignored. Elementary schools routinely allot as little as 45 minutes a week to Social Studies. What meaningful teaching and learning can happen in only 45 minutes a week? Middle and high schools allow more scheduled time, but frequently subtract from that time by scheduling things such as pep rallies, school assemblies, and fundraising meetings during Social Studies classes. These practices send a clear picture to students that Social Studies, when it is not tested, is less important to the school than tested subjects.

When Social Studies is tested, teachers face a different problem: too much to teach in the time they have. This often leads teachers to engage in "inch deep and mile wide" teaching practices. Compounding this time problem is the fact that students usually come to Social Studies with little to no familiarity with the content. Teachers then spend considerable time on repetitive, "drill and kill" teaching practices in the hope they will help students to retain information at least until testing day. While many teachers would like to engage students in more meaningful activities, they often do not feel they have time for it. According to one high school history teacher in a study by Kenneth Vogler (2005),

> I use the entire academic year preparing my students for the United States history subject exam. My choice of instructional delivery and materials is completely dependent on preparation for this test. Therefore, I do not use current events, long-term projects, or creative group/corporate work because this is not tested and the delivery format is not used. All my tests reflect the testing format of the subject area tests – multiple-choice and open ended questions (p. 19).

Some researchers claim that mandated accountability exams lead to a "just the facts, ma'am" approach to teaching social studies (Vogler & Virtue, 2007). Other researchers go further and contend that "because multiple-choice testing leads to multiple-choice teaching, the methods that teachers have in their arsenal become reduced, and teaching work is deskilled" (Smith, 1991, p. 10).

Another reason Social Studies is hard to teach is that teachers have so few models of good Social Studies teaching. Most Social Studies teaching takes the form of "telling," in which teachers lecture, i.e. "tell" students information, perhaps show a picture or video, and then test students on the content. In this paradigm, students are not asked to actively learn, only to passively retain information. A simple reason explains this: teachers usually teach the way their teachers taught them. High schools and universities are notorious for this kind of passive teaching and learning. So, it makes sense that teachers continue to use these methods. The problem is that they just don't work that well if thinking is the goal.

Lastly, finding and using quality resources presents an ongoing challenge to Social Studies teachers. Textbooks are the most commonly used resource. This makes sense. Almost all classrooms have them, and they present information through efficient explanations, pictures, charts, and other visual methods. And teachers do not need to go looking for them, which may be the biggest benefit of all. Yet, textbooks contain a number of problems too: they usually present surface-level understandings; their reading level is often too high for students; and they always contain unaddressed bias. Further, and perhaps most important, they do a bad job of presenting multiple perspectives about issues and events. Teachers, then, need to find resources on their own that can offer students more depth and more varied perspectives. These other types of resources exist. Libraries and museums will often loan entire boxes of varied materials to teachers. Nonprofits and NGOs sometimes provide materials about specific topics. And the Internet, of course, is awash in historical information. The challenge for teachers is creating the time to acquire these resources and learning how to use them, especially when teachers are so often overwhelmed by the other responsibilities of their jobs.

Even with all of these challenges, quality teaching in Social Studies is crucial. **Social studies helps to create a literate public that cares about social and historical issues, that can analyze problems through context, and that has a global awareness of the challenges facing society.** To create such a public, students must be presented with meaningful problems and asked to engage in analytical thinking. Forty-five minutes a week of Social Studies won't cut it, nor will a reductionist focus on test scores or teaching methods that keep students disengaged. Teachers face significant challenges in teaching Social Studies. But the urgency to confront those challenges in order to create this much needed public has never been greater.

Our essay is pretty good. But there is at least one sentence that we can change according to the points made in this step. Actually, we've already edited it some in Step 11. Here it is:

- Social studies helps to create a literate public that cares about social and historical issues, that can analyze problems through context, and that has a global awareness of the challenges facing society.

Do you see the problem? I don't write "I believe," so that's not it. It's not too wordy. The sentences uses a lot of words, but it makes a complicated point. Look at the list. I'll put it in bold for you:

- Social Studies helps to create a literate public **that cares** about social and historical issues, **that can analyze** problems through context, and **that has a global awareness** of the challenges facing society.

The problem is that this list is not parallel. The first verb, "cares," is in simple and active voice. But the other two are not active. The sentence should like this:

- Social Studies helps to create a literate public **that cares** about social and historical issues, **that analyzes** problems through context, and **that addresses** the challenges facing a global society.

Now the sentence is parallel. Notice how much better this new version sounds than the original? Our essay is now ready to go. Go back through your essay and study it for wordiness, for parallelism, and for any "I believe" statements. Also, please use our sample essay as a model for doing all of these steps.

Finished Sample Essay:

"The Difficulty of Teaching Social Studies in Elementary Classrooms."

Teaching social studies is hard. Teachers face a variety of obstacles that can make their job feel impossible. Standardized testing creates significant pressure on teachers. State and school district curriculum plans often ask too much of teachers and students: teach and learn too much content in too short of a time frame. This lack of time can pressure teachers to teach just facts. Sometimes social studies isn't tested, so it gets ignored for tested subjects that "matter." Yet, even when Social Studies is tested, those scores do not always fully count towards a school's accountability rating. Models of quality teaching can also be in short supply in Social Studies. Further, teachers often face a lack of resources to meaningfully teach Social Studies.

Teachers constantly struggle with a lack of time to teach. Standardized testing plays a crucial role in this time problem. When Social Studies is not tested, it tends to get ignored. Elementary schools routinely allot as little as 45 minutes a week to Social Studies. What meaningful teaching and learning can happen in only 45 minutes a week? Middle and high schools allow more scheduled time, but frequently subtract from that time by scheduling things such as pep rallies, school assemblies, and fundraising meetings during Social

Studies classes. These practices send a clear picture to students that Social Studies, when it is not tested, is less important to the school than tested subjects.

When Social Studies is tested, teachers face a different problem: too much to teach in the time they have. This often leads teachers to engage in "inch deep and mile wide" teaching practices. Compounding this time problem is the fact that students usually come to Social Studies with little to no familiarity with the content. Teachers then spend considerable time on repetitive, "drill and kill" teaching practices in the hope they will help students to retain information at least until testing day. While many teachers would like to engage students in more meaningful activities, they often do not feel they have time for it. According to one high school history teacher in a study by Kenneth Vogler (2005),

> I use the entire academic year preparing my students for the United States history subject exam. My choice of instructional delivery and materials is completely dependent on preparation for this test. Therefore, I do not use current events, long-term projects, or creative group/corporate work because this is not tested and the delivery format is not used. All my tests reflect the testing format of the subject area tests – multiple-choice and open ended questions (p. 19).

Some researchers claim that mandated accountability exams lead to a "just the facts, ma'am" approach to teaching social studies (Vogler & Virtue, 2007). Other researchers go further and contend that "because multiple-choice testing leads to multiple-choice teaching, the methods that teachers have in their arsenal become reduced, and teaching work is deskilled" (Smith, 1991, p. 10).

Another reason Social Studies is hard to teach is that teachers have so few models of good Social Studies teaching. Most Social Studies teaching takes the form of "telling," in which teachers lecture, i.e. "tell" students information, perhaps show a picture or video, and then test students on the content. In this paradigm, students are not asked to actively learn, only to passively retain information. A simple reason explains this: teachers usually teach the way their teachers taught them. High schools and universities are notorious for this kind of passive teaching and learning. So, it makes sense that teachers continue to use these methods. The problem is that they just don't work that well if thinking is the goal.

Lastly, finding and using quality resources presents an ongoing challenge to Social Studies teachers. Textbooks are the most commonly used resource. This makes sense. Almost all classrooms have them, and they present information through efficient explanations, pictures, charts, and other visual methods. And teachers do not need to go looking for them, which may be the biggest benefit of all. Yet, textbooks contain a number of problems too: they usually present surface-level understandings; their reading level is often too high for students; and they always contain unaddressed bias. Further, and perhaps most important, they do a bad job of presenting multiple perspectives about issues and events. Teachers, then, need to find resources on their own that can offer students more depth and more varied perspectives. These other types of resources exist. Libraries and museums will often loan entire boxes of varied materials to teachers. Nonprofits and NGOs sometimes provide materials about specific topics. And the Internet, of course, is awash in historical information. The challenge for teachers is creating the time to acquire these resources and learning how to use them, especially when teachers are so often overwhelmed by the other responsibilities of their jobs.

Even with all of these challenges, quality teaching in Social Studies is crucial. Social Studies helps to create a literate public that cares about social and historical issues, that analyzes problems through context, and that addresses the challenges facing a global society. To create such a public, students must be presented with meaningful problems and asked to engage in analytical thinking. Forty-five minutes a week of Social Studies won't cut it, nor will a reductionist focus on test scores or teaching methods that keep students disengaged. Teachers face significant challenges in teaching Social Studies. But the urgency to confront those challenges in order to create this much needed public has never been greater.

We've finished all of the steps. Study them, follow them, and practice them and your writing will improve tremendously. And remember to do them in order. Each step is important and, put together, they take the guesswork out of writing.

BONUS: USE CITATIONS LIKE A PRO

When, Where, and How Often to Use Citations

Why Use Citations?

Think of academic writing as a big conversation. When professors or other academics publish in academic journals, they are joining a conversation with other academics about that particular topic, whether the paper is about engineering, chemistry, literature, or anything else. They have to acknowledge what other people have written about the topic. This creates a context for their paper – what their paper is about and how it connects to what other people have written about the topic. Sometimes academics will agree with other studies; sometimes they will disagree. Doing this helps authors answer the "so what?" question: why is this study important? What does it have to do with what people already know or think about a topic? How is the study new, or how does it offer a new way of thinking about a topic? We have to establish what knowledge already exists before we can add to or change that knowledge.

Another reason that academics use citations is to support claims that they make. For example, say I want to make a claim about education or training programs for inmates or for young children. Well, I would need some actual facts to back up my claim. Or say I want to state that homework is or isn't beneficial for kindergarten students. Again, I would need to cite some studies that have the hard data to support my claim.

So, why do you have to do all of this if you're not writing for publication? Because in writing academic papers, you're working as a sort of an academic-in-training so you have to follow the practices that academics do. You need to create contexts for your arguments and you need to support claims that you make.

Where Should I Use Citations?

You will usually use citations in the beginning of the essay, when you are establishing the problem that you're writing about, as well as towards the end, when you are discussing your data or your analysis of the problem/issue. You usually won't use citations when you are presenting information or data about your topic. However, this isn't a strict rule. Say you are discussing an author's use of imagery. As you analyze that use of imagery, you might want to compare it to other examples of writing. You would cite those other sources. Another place you probably wouldn't use citations is in the conclusion. It's possible that you would want to cite, say, a study or some statistics, but that isn't common.

How Often Should I Use Citations?

You use citations for support: to support claims that you make, facts that you present, to create a context, to give background knowledge, etc. So, you probably won't need to use them that much. Remember that most of the writing needs to be your words and your thoughts.

Cite Correctly…and with Style

There are two main ways to cite sources in academic writing: either cite a paraphrased point or cite a section of a sentence, an entire sentence, or several sentences.

Paraphrasing

Let's start with paraphrasing. Look at this short passage. It's the opening paragraph of a long journal article:

> "There is an ongoing effort by researchers to better understand the influences on teachers' work. Teachers' work can be shaped by a range of factors, such as teacher education programs, the types of students on teaches, teachers' milieu, teachers' knowledge and beliefs, and mandated accountability testing. Researchers have studied teachers' work in a variety of ways, for example in terms of teachers' roles (Valli & Buese, 2007), teachers' workload (Easthope & Easthope, 2000), teachers' teaching practices (Wills, 2007; Wills & Sandholtz, 2009), and teachers' knowledge (Craig, 2004, 2013)."

In that paragraph, I begin to establish the problem that I'm writing about. At the end of the paragraph, I make a series of factual claims which I need to back up. My citations do that for me. I just need to cite one or more studies to support each claim, in this case about research on teachers' roles, teachers' workload, teachers' teaching practices, and teachers' knowledge. All I have to do is insert the author and year of each paper I want to cite. These are very short paraphrases, in that all they do is state a broad category.

Another way to paraphrase is to use specific points from other papers. Check out the passage below:

> These frailties are intimately bound in context, and researchers must form relationships and invest themselves into those contexts as they seek truer truths about people's experiences that, yes, may link to theory but are not necessarily about theory. McLaren (1992) called this preparing to be wounded in the field, in that researchers must put at risk their habitual ways of self-construction. McLaren's phrasing resonates; to be blinded by self can blur broader vision. But here I reach for something deeper, more akin to narrative notions of relationship and the stories educators live and tell about themselves in context (Connelly & Clandinin, 1990).

The first sentence is making a point about something that researchers must do. The second sentence is used to support that point. It paraphrases something that a different scholar wrote (in this case someone named McLaren). The third sentence comments on the paraphrased point in sentence two. And the fourth sentence paraphrases yet another point (something from the writers Connelly and Clandinin).

Let's look more closely at the two paraphrased points. In the second sentence, the paraphrased point is "preparing to be wounded in the field." It is set up by the simple phrase "McLaren (1992) called this...." In the fourth sentence, the paraphrased point is "narrative notions of relationship and the stories educators live and tell about themselves in context." This last point is set up with the words "more akin to..." These are good examples of blending a cited paraphrasing into the paper. Blending a citation into the surrounding sentences is crucial if you want to cite well. You don't want it to stick out. In terms of punctuation, remember that the period goes *after* parentheses, but *before* quotation marks.

Using Sentences or Phrases

The importance of blending language is especially true when citing all or part of a sentence. You'll almost never see good academic writing that just throws a quoted sentence into the middle of a paragraph. Instead, good writers embed their quotations. Here's an example of what *not* to do:

> The population of English language learners (ELLs) has rapidly increased, therefore making it very difficult for ELLs to get the proper education. "Georgia reports that ELLs in public schools increased by 650 percent during the same period (Batt, Kim, and Sunderman, 2005). Clearly, public school teachers throughout the nation will face a greater influx of immigrant children." (Brown, 2007).

There are a number of problems with this passage. First, it's hard to know what is being quoted and from where. The closing quotation marks after 'children' make it seem as if both sentences are being quoted. But from where? The student included a citation for each sentence. Did she just mean to cite two whole sentences in a row? Or did she mean that the first sentence was quoted within the same source as the second sentence? So, that is unclear. Also, the essay isn't about Georgia. Yet, beginning the second sentence like that implies that the paper *is* about Georgia. Third, the order of sentences 2 and 3 is wrong. Sentence 2 should come after sentence 3, since it can serve as an example of the point that sentence 3 makes. Fourth, if you're going to cite sentences or phrases, you need to include the page number in the citation (this student didn't include them, so I'll have to leave them out). I'm going to also change up some of the language. Here is a revised version of that passage:

> The population of English language learners (ELLs) has rapidly increased, making it difficult for those students to get a proper education. Brown (2007) claims that "public school teachers throughout the nation will face a greater influx of immigrant children." For example, the state of "Georgia reports that ELLs in public schools [has] increased by 650%" (Batt, Kim, & Sunderman, 2005).

Notice how much easier this revised passage is to follow. You can think about arranging the argument like this:

1. Number of ELLs in public schools is increasing
2. One researcher stated that teachers across the nation will see more immigrant students (this statement supports the first sentence)
3. An example from a study about Georgia that supports the second sentence

Instead of just throwing in whole sentences or phrases, I blended them into the other sentences. I wrote that "Brown (2007) claims that..." and "For example, the state of...."

Let's look at one more example of what not to do and revise it into something better. It's actually the next 4 sentences from the same student's essay:

> Teachers are greatly affected by the amount of ELLs they have in their classrooms. They have to get to know their students and understanding their backgrounds. "Many teachers have a wide variety of cultures and languages represented in their classrooms. This presents a challenge in communicating with students and understanding their cultures." (Hansen, 2007)

The quoted sentences break up the flow of the sentences, and they kind of feel like a repeat of what was just written. There is no introduction or context made for the quotation; it's just tossed in there. Here's a revised version of that passage:

> Teachers can be affected by the number of ELLs they have in their classrooms. Because "many teachers have a wide variety of cultures and languages represented in their classrooms[, this] presents [them with] a challenge in communicating with students and understanding their cultures" (Hansen, 2007). This can make it difficult for teachers to get to know their students.

Let's go sentence by sentence. In sentence 1, I changed "are" to "can be," because we don't know that all teachers are affected by the number of ELLs. But we do know, from the citation in sentence 2, that teachers "can be" affected by the number of ELLs. I switched sentences 2, 3, and 4 because they work better in this order. I moved the original sentence 2 to the end, because that sentence illustrates an example of how this challenge can affect teachers.

Notice also how I embedded the quotation. It's ok to change a capitalized letter. It's also ok to use what was a complete sentence as a part of a new sentence: Because "many teachers have…" I just added a few words to shape my sentence to a form that flows better. I also changed the way the two quoted sentences fit together; what were two sentences became one long sentence. Since I took out the period, added a comma, and changed "This" to "this," I needed to do that with brackets. Brackets show what I added to a quoted sentence. I'll put both of the student's original passages together so you can see what the whole thing originally looked like:

> The population of English language learners (ELLs) has rapidly increased, therefore making it very difficult for ELLs to get the proper education. "Georgia reports that ELLs in public schools increased by 650 percent during the same period (Batt, Kim, and Sunderman, 2005). Clearly, public school teachers throughout the nation will face a greater influx of immigrant children." (Brown, 2007). Teachers are greatly affected by the amount of ELLs they have in their classrooms. They have to get to know their students and understanding their backgrounds. "Many teachers have a wide variety of cultures and languages represented in their classrooms. This presents a challenge in communicating with students and understanding their cultures." (Hansen, 2007)

The student has presented some information, and we can mostly make sense of it. But some of it is unclear, and it doesn't flow well at all. Now look at the revised version. This revised version flows much more smoothly and presents information in a way that is easier to understand:

The population of English language learners (ELLs) has rapidly increased, making it difficult for those students to get a proper education. Brown (2007) claims that "public school teachers throughout the nation will face a greater influx of immigrant children." For example, the state of "Georgia reports that [the number of] ELLs in public schools [has] increased by 650%" (Batt, Kim, & Sunderman, 2005). Teachers can be affected by the number of ELLs they have in their classrooms. Because "many teachers have a wide variety of cultures and languages represented in their classrooms[, this] presents [them with] a challenge in communicating with students and understanding their cultures" (Hansen, 2007). This can make it difficult for teachers to get to know their students.

Let's take a look at another example, this time trying to decide which part of a sentence to cite. We'll start with the following two sentences:

1. "Best practice" would seem to be the pinnacle of practice to generate learning inside the classroom.
2. The notion of a best practice can seem especially compelling.

In the first sentence, I state something about 'best practice,' and in the second sentence I state that it's compelling. However, I haven't defined what best practice means. But look, I found a sentence that defines best practice: "One line of thinking about this question uses the term best practices, borrowed from the business world to refer to a set of techniques for most efficiently and effectively producing a desired outcome." I obviously can't use that whole sentence, though. It's too long and just doesn't fit. Besides, if I put it in, the paragraph would look like this:

"Best practice" would seem to be the pinnacle of practice to generate learning inside the classroom. "One line of thinking about this question uses the term best practices, borrowed from the business world to refer to a set of techniques for most efficiently and effectively producing a desired outcome" (Lampert 25). The notion of a best practice can seem especially compelling.

Here's a better way to do it. You don't have to use the whole sentence; just use what you need. Try this:

> "Best practice" would seem to be the pinnacle of practice to generate learning inside the classroom. Borrowed from the language of business, it refers "to a set of techniques for most efficiently and effectively producing a desired outcome" (Lampert 25), suggesting assurance for the educator, legislator, or parent wondering about what to do to improve learning in schools. The notion of a best practice can seem especially compelling.

I paraphrased the opening of the second sentence and used "it refers" to tell readers that this is a definition. I also added some analysis at the end of the second sentence.

Create a Reference List and do In-text Citations

How to Make a Reference List

There are a variety of citation systems. The two most common ones for students are probably MLA and APA. MLA stands for the Modern Language Association, and APA stands for the American Psychological Association. These two organizations have created a system for referencing sources (as well as other aspects of writing). You might need to know how to create a reference list using each system. It's easy. Here are examples of the three most commonly cited types of sources for academic papers. When you make your list, make it alphabetically by authors' last names. If you have multiple sources for the same author, then list those chronologically beginning with the earliest date.

MLA

Journal article

    Format: Author. "Title of the Article." *Name of Journal.* Volume.number (year published): page range.

    Example: Neumann, Jacob W. "Critical Pedagogy and Faith." *Educational Theory.* 61.5 (2011): 601-619.

Book

> Format: Author. *Title of Book.* City where published: Publisher, year published.
>
> Example: Agar, Michael H. *The Professional Stranger: An Informal Introduction to Ethnography.* San Diego, CA: Academic Press, Inc, 1980.

Chapter in an edited book

> Format: Author. "Chapter Title." *Title of Book.* Ed [Editor]. Name (First Last). City where published: Publisher, year published. page range.
>
> Example: Neumann, Jacob W. "Bilingual education, culture, and the challenge of developing Freirean dispositions in teacher education." *Paulo Freire: The global legacy.* Ed. Michael Peters and Tina Besley. New York: Peter Lang, 2014. 431-443.

Here's what you do in MLA if you have multiple authors:

> For one author, you write it "Neumann, Jacob W."
>
> For two authors, you write it "Neumann, Jacob W. and John Smith."
>
> For three or more authors, you write it "Neumann, Jacob W., John Smith, and Bill Thomas."

APA

Journal article

> Format: Author. (Year published.). Title of article. *Title of Journal, volume*(number), pages.
>
> Example: Neumann, J. W. (2011). Critical pedagogy and faith. *Educational Theory, 61*(5), 601-19.

Book

> Format: Author. (Year published.). *Title of book.* City where published: Publisher.

Example: Agar, M. H. (1980). *The professional stranger: An informal introduction to ethnography.* San Diego, CA: Academic Press, Inc.

Chapter in an edited book

Format: Author. (Year published). Title of chapter. In (name of editor or editors) (Ed. or Eds.), Title of book (page numbers). City where published: Publisher.

Example: Neumann, J. W. (2014). Bilingual education, culture, and the challenge of developing Freirean dispositions in teacher education. In M. A. Peters & T. Besley (Eds.), *Paulo Freire: The global legacy* (pp. 431-443). New York: Peter Lang.

Here's what you do in APA if you have multiple authors:

For one author, you write it "Neumann, J. W."

For two authors, you write it "Neumann, J. W., & Smith, J."

For three or more authors, you write it "Neumann, J. W., Smith, J., & Thomas, B."

How to Do In-Text Citations

In-text citations let your readers know which points, either paraphrased or quoted, you found in other sources. MLA and APA have different systems for identifying citations within an essay.

For paraphrasing

Here is an example in MLA format that shows in-text citations for paraphrasing. In MLA, you just cite the author(s) for a paraphrased citation:

Researchers have studied teachers' work in a variety of ways, for example in terms of teachers' roles (Valli and Buese), teachers' workload (Easthope and Easthope), teachers' teaching practices (Wills; Will and Sandholtz), and teachers' knowledge (Craig).

This is what the same passage looks like in APA. In APA, you cite the author(s) and the year the source was published:

Researchers have studied teachers' work in a variety of ways, for example in terms of teachers' roles (Valli & Buese, 2007), teachers' workload (Easthope & Easthope, 2000), teachers' teaching practices (Wills, 2007; Will & Sandholtz, 2009), and teachers' knowledge (Craig, 2004).

Here's another example of a paraphrase in MLA. In this example, there is no need to cite the author's name, since it's mentioned in the sentence. Instead, you just identify part of the title of the source, in this case "Life" means "Life in Schools:"

McLaren called this preparing to be wounded in the field, in that researchers must put at risk their habitual ways of self-construction ("Life").

Here's what that same sentence looks like in APA. You'll notice that I also did not cite the author's name, since it's mentioned in the sentence. But this time I list the year the source was published. You'll also notice that I put the (1992) right after the author's name. This is a common practice in APA, but it's also ok to list put the year at the end of the sentence. I put it at the end because that way readers who are familiar with McLaren's work will know right away which publication it is:

McLaren (1992) called this preparing to be wounded in the field, in that researchers must put at risk their habitual ways of self-construction.

For sentences and phrases
In-text citations for sentences and phrases are slightly different. You include the page number because you want to show where in the text you found the quotation. You can also structure the citation somewhat differently than for paraphrasing. I'll explain. Here's an example of a phrase quoted using MLA:

According to White, social education is about "social efficacy, empowerment, and emancipation" (42).

Because the author's name (White) is in the sentence, you just list the page number after the quoted phrase. This works if there is only one work by this author in your reference list. But if you use two works by this author in the reference list, you will need to give readers information about which work I used:

> According to White, social education is about "social efficacy, empowerment, and emancipation" (*Social Justice* 42).

In this example, "Social Justice" is short for the title of the book, *Social Justice in Teacher Education*. You follow this with the page number. Now, if the source was a journal article, then you would not italicize the title, but put it in quotes ("Social Justice" 42).

The same sentence can be cited multiple ways in APA. You can put the year and page number at the end:

> According to White, social education is about "social efficacy, empowerment, and emancipation" (2011, p. 42).

Or you can put the year after the author's name and the page number at the end. This is my favorite method. I don't have to wait until the end of the sentence to know which publication this is by White, and the (2011) just after White gives me a longer pause at the comma. I think it sounds kind of awkward to just state "According to White, social education...." I prefer the longer pause in "According to White (2011), social education…:"

> According to White (2011), social education is about "social efficacy, empowerment, and emancipation" (p. 42).

You can also cite a sentence as support for a point you have been making. Check this out in MLA:

> As Carspecken put it, "we use our research, in fact, to refine social theory rather than merely to describe social life" (3).

Here's what it looks like in APA. First, date and page number at the end:

> As Carspecken put it, "we use our research, in fact, to refine social theory rather than merely to describe social life" (1996, p. 3).

Now, with the date right after the author's name and the page number at the end. This example shows the ways most academic writers structure their quotations within a paper:

> As Carspecken (1996) put it, "we use our research, in fact, to refine social theory rather than merely to describe social life" (p. 3).

In the cited book, the sentence begins with "we:" "We use our research…." It's ok to make the first word lowercase so that it reads like a phrase: As Carspecken (1996) put it, "we use our research…."

AVOIDING PLAGIARISM

Simply put, plagiarism means taking somebody else's work and passing it off as your own. Borrowing a whole paragraph or even a sentence and pretending it is yours is plagiarism. You pretend it's yours by not citing it. If you cite it, it's not plagiarism. However, sometimes it's hard to know whether you should cite something or not. When in doubt, cite it in the text. You also cannot just change a few words of a passage and call it your own. That's still plagiarism. To paraphrase something, you need to change most of the words to your own words. Take the following sentence from a journal article:

> "One line of thinking about this question uses the term best practices, borrowed from the business world to refer to a set of techniques for most efficiently and effectively producing a desired outcome" (Lampert 25).

Say I rewrote the sentence and just changed a few words:

> "The term best practices is borrowed from the business world and refers to a set of techniques for most efficiently and effectively producing a desired outcome."

This would be plagiarism if you didn't cite it, at least in my classes. The sentence is basically the same; the last part is word-for-word the same. What about this sentence?:

> "Best practices refers to actions that efficiently produce desired results."

This would be a paraphrase, and it would still need a brief citation. It's still pretty specific and contains multiple elements (actions and desired results).

However, if we chop it down even more, we might not need to cite it:

> "Best practices are aimed towards desired results."

This example wouldn't be plagiarism and wouldn't require citations. We've removed several elements (the business world, efficiency, a set of techniques, actions). But I'd probably cite it anyway, because the citation gives the sentence more weight and authority.

QUICK GUIDE TO WRITING YOUR ESSAY

This section shows you a brief outline of how to build your essay. It doesn't give the same thorough explanations and examples that the rest of the book does, but it will give you a quick picture of how the process works. When you write an essay, you are in effect building that essay, putting it together section by section and piece by piece. This short guide gives you an overview of how that process works. I show you how it works by using the sample essay that we build in the book, only without all of the elaboration and explanation. Be sure to notice how I start with the big picture and work my way towards the details.

1. Outline the ideas/points you might want to make in the essay. Don't try to get it exactly right the first time, just get down your thoughts.

Sample topic: "The difficulty of teaching Social Studies in elementary classrooms"

Sample outline
Standardized testing
Pressure to teach just facts
Lack to time
Schools focus on reading, etc
Does it even count?
Too much content – what to teach?
Lack of resources

2. Write a thesis sentence for your essay. This sentence should cover all of the points you list in your outline. Again, don't try to get it perfect right now; you can always change it later. Keep the language as simple as possible. Don't try to be fancy. Just be direct.

Thesis sentence: Teachers face a variety of obstacles that can make their job feel impossible.

3. Write topic sentences for each body paragraph in your essay. Be clear and direct, using simple language. After thinking about my outline, I decide to change the

order. I'll list the new paragraph order, and then below it write the topic sentences for each paragraph.

New outline of body paragraphs
Paragraph: Standardized testing
            Lack of time
Paragraph: Pressure to teach facts
Paragraph: Does it even count?
            Schools focus on reading, math, etc
Paragraph: Too much content
Paragraph: Lack of resources

Topic sentences for each body paragraph
Paragraph: Standardized testing shapes, and often limits, how Social
            Studies is taught.

Paragraph: Standardized testing often creates an intense pressure to
            teach just facts.

Paragraph: The focus on tested subjects can de-emphasize Social
            Studies, since it often is not tested.

Paragraph: The sprawling nature of Social Studies content can also
            impact how it is taught.

Paragraph: Finally, a lack of resources can strain Social Studies
            teaching.

4. Write your introduction. Be sure your introduction does 3 things: 1) it establishes a context for your essay; 2) it clearly states what the essay is about (this is your thesis sentence); and 3) it gives readers a sense of the points you'll be making in the essay. Don't try to create a "hook." Just do these three things and you'll create an effective introduction. I recommend doing them in this order. So you can see all three components, I'll put the context (#1 from our list) in bold; I'll underline the thesis sentence (#2); and I'll italicize the points I'm going to make (#3). After the introduction, I'll list the topic sentences for the body paragraphs so you can see the essay being built.

Introduction: Teaching social studies is hard. **Teachers face a variety of obstacles that can make their job feel impossible.** Standardized testing creates significant pressure on teachers. State and school district curriculum plans often ask too much of teachers and students: teach and learn too much content in a too short time frame. This lack of time can pressure teachers to teach just facts. Sometimes social studies isn't tested, so it gets ignored for tested subjects that "matter." Even when social studies is tested, those scores do not always fully count towards a school's accountability rating. Further, teachers often face a lack of resources to meaningfully teach Social Studies.

Paragraph 2: Standardized testing shapes, and often limits, how Social Studies is taught.

Paragraph 3: Standardized testing often creates an intense pressure to teach just facts.

Paragraph 4: The focus on tested subjects can de-emphasize Social Studies, since it often is not tested.

Paragraph 5: The sprawling nature of Social Studies content can also impact how it is taught.

Paragraph 6: Finally, a lack of resources can strain Social Studies teaching.

5. Write your body paragraphs. The topic sentences that you have already written will be either the first or second (and occasionally the third) sentence in the paragraph. When you write these paragraphs, you might find that you want to rewrite one or more of your topic sentences. You'll see that I changed most of my original topic sentences. I even deleted one of my body paragraph ideas (what was paragraph 5 – about sprawling content) and put it into the second body paragraph (paragraph 3). Don't get confused by this. It's part of the writing process, so don't be afraid to do this. I'll highlight the thesis and topic sentences. Also, remember that if you use or reference information that you found in specific sources, you need to cite them, especially if you're writing any type of research paper. Most of the

information in these example paragraphs I know through my work in schools, so I don't need to cite it. But you will see me cite two articles I used as support in paragraph 3.

Introduction: Teaching social studies is hard. **Teachers face a variety of obstacles that can make their job feel impossible.** Standardized testing creates significant pressure on teachers. State and school district curriculum plans often ask too much of teachers and students: teach and learn too much content in a too short time frame. This lack of time can pressure teachers to teach just facts. Sometimes social studies isn't tested, so it gets ignored for tested subjects that "matter." Even when social studies is tested, those scores do not always fully count towards a school's accountability rating. Further, teachers often face a lack of resources to meaningfully teach Social Studies.

Paragraph 2:   Teachers constantly struggle with a lack of time to teach. **Standardized testing plays a crucial role in this time problem.** When Social Studies is not tested, it tends to get ignored. Elementary schools routinely allot as little as 45 minutes a week to Social Studies. What meaningful teaching and learning can happen in only 45 minutes a week? Middle and high schools allow more scheduled time, but frequently subtract from that time by scheduling things such as pep rallies, school assemblies, and fundraising meetings during Social Studies classes. These practices send a clear picture to students that Social Studies, when it is not tested, is less important to the school than tested subjects.

Paragraph 3:   **When Social Studies is tested, teachers face a different problem: too much to teach in the time they have.** This often leads teachers to engage in "inch deep and mile wide" teaching practices. Compounding this time problem is the fact that students usually come to Social Studies with little to no familiarity with the content. Teachers then spend considerable time on repetitive, "drill and kill" teaching practices in the hope they will help students to retain information at least until testing day. While many teachers would like to engage students in more meaningful activities, they often do not feel they have time for it. According to one high school history teacher in a study by Kenneth Vogler (2005),

> I use the entire academic year preparing my students for the United States history subject exam. My choice of instructional delivery and materials is completely dependent on preparation for this test. Therefore, I do not use current events, long-term projects, or creative group/corporate work because this is not tested and the delivery format is not used. All my tests reflect the testing format of the subject area tests – multiple-choice and open ended questions (p. 19).

Some researchers claim that mandated accountability exams lead to a "just the facts, ma'am" approach to teaching social studies (Vogler & Virtue, 2007). Other researchers go further and contend that "because multiple-choice testing leads to multiple-choice teaching, the methods that teachers have in their arsenal become reduced, and teaching work is deskilled" (Smith, 1991, p. 10).

Paragraph 4: **Another reason Social Studies is hard to teach is that teachers have so few models of good Social Studies teaching.** Most Social Studies teaching takes the form of "telling," in which teachers lecture, i.e. "tell" students information, perhaps show a picture or video, and then test students on the content. In this paradigm, students are not asked to actively learn, only to passively retain information. There is a simple reason for this: teachers usually teach the way they were taught when they were students. High schools and universities are notorious for this kind of passive teaching and learning. So, it makes sense that teachers continue to use these methods. The problem is that they just don't work that well if thinking is the goal.

Paragraph 5:   **Lastly, finding and using quality resources presents an ongoing challenge to Social Studies teachers.** Textbooks are the most commonly used resource. This makes sense. Almost all classrooms have them, and they present information through efficient explanations, pictures, charts, and other visual methods. And teachers do not need to go looking for them, which may be the biggest benefit of all. Yet, textbooks contain a number of problems too: they usually present surface-level understandings; their reading level is often too high for students; and they always contain unaddressed bias. Further, and perhaps most important, they do a bad job of presenting multiple perspectives about issues and events. Teachers, then, need to find resources on their own that can offer students more depth and more varied perspectives. These other types of resources exist. Libraries and museums will often loan entire boxes of varied materials to teachers. Nonprofits and NGOs sometimes provide materials about specific topics. And the Internet, of course, is awash in historical information. The challenge for teachers is creating the time to acquire these resources and learning how to use them, especially when teachers are so often overwhelmed by the other responsibilities of their jobs.

6. Write a concluding paragraph. Be sure the conclusion connects to your introduction. They form a pair that must fit together. Make sure the last sentence in your conclusion somehow goes with the first sentence in your introduction. Here's the conclusion to our sample essay:

Even with all of these challenges, quality teaching in Social Studies is crucial. Social Studies helps to create a public that is literate about social and historical issues, can analyze problems through context, and has a global awareness of the challenges facing society. To create such a public, students must be presented with meaningful problems and asked to engage in analytical thinking. Forty-five minutes a week of Social Studies won't cut it, nor will a reductionist focus on test scores or teaching methods that keep students disengaged. Teachers face significant challenges in teaching Social Studies. But the urgency to confront those challenges in order to create this much needed public has never been greater.

7. Edit your essay. Be sure that you read your writing out loud to yourself. Your ears catch what your eyes miss. This is the best and easiest editing trick you can do. While editing your essay, it is crucial that you do the following things:

- Include only one idea in each body paragraph
- Use effective transitions
- Write in complete sentences
- Keep your writing parallel
- Pay attention to your verbs
- Eliminate wordiness

8. Put your essay together. Here's the full sample essay. It's not long, but it will demonstrate all of our points.

"The Difficulty of Teaching Social Studies in Elementary Classrooms"

Teaching social studies is hard. Teachers face a variety of obstacles that can make their job feel impossible. Standardized testing creates significant pressure on teachers. State and school district curriculum plans often ask too much of teachers and students: teach and learn too much content in too short of a time frame. This lack of time can pressure teachers to teach just facts. Sometimes social studies isn't tested, so it gets ignored for tested subjects that "matter." Yet, even when Social Studies is tested, those scores do not always fully count towards a school's accountability rating. Models of quality teaching can also be in short supply in Social Studies. Further, teachers often face a lack of resources to meaningfully teach Social Studies.

Teachers constantly struggle with a lack of time to teach. Standardized testing plays a crucial role in this time problem. When Social Studies is not tested, it tends to get ignored. Elementary schools routinely allot as little as 45 minutes a week to Social Studies. What meaningful teaching and learning can happen in only 45 minutes a week? Middle and high schools allow more scheduled time, but frequently subtract from that time by scheduling things such as pep rallies, school assemblies, and fundraising meetings during Social Studies classes. These practices send a clear picture to students that Social Studies, when it is not tested, is less important to the school than tested subjects.

When Social Studies is tested, teachers face a different problem: too much to teach in the time they have. This often leads teachers to engage in "inch deep and mile wide" teaching practices. Compounding this time problem is the fact that students usually come to Social Studies with little to no familiarity with the content. Teachers then spend considerable time on repetitive, "drill and kill" teaching practices in the hope they will help students to retain information at least until testing day. While many teachers would like to engage students in more meaningful activities, they often do not feel they have time for it. According to one high school history teacher in a study by Kenneth Vogler (2005),

> I use the entire academic year preparing my students for the United States history subject exam. My choice of instructional delivery and materials is completely dependent on preparation for this test. Therefore, I do not use current events, long-term projects, or creative group/corporate work because this is not tested and the delivery format is not used. All my tests reflect the testing format of the subject area tests – multiple-choice and open ended questions (p. 19).

Some researchers claim that mandated accountability exams lead to a "just the facts, ma'am" approach to teaching social studies (Vogler & Virtue, 2007). Other researchers go further and contend that "because multiple-choice testing leads to multiple-choice teaching, the methods that teachers have in their arsenal become reduced, and teaching work is deskilled" (Smith, 1991, p. 10).

Another reason Social Studies is hard to teach is that teachers have so few models of good Social Studies teaching. Most Social Studies teaching takes the form of "telling," in which teachers lecture, i.e. "tell" students information, perhaps show a picture or video, and then test students on the content. In this paradigm, students are not asked to actively learn, only to passively retain information. There is a simple reason for this: teachers usually teach the way they were taught when they were students. High schools and universities are notorious for this kind of passive teaching and learning. So, it makes sense that teachers continue to use these methods. The problem is that they just don't work that well if thinking is the goal.

Lastly, finding and using quality resources presents an ongoing challenge to Social Studies teachers. Textbooks are the most commonly used resource. This makes sense. Almost all classrooms have them, and they present information through efficient explanations, pictures, charts, and other visual methods. And teachers do not need to go looking for them, which may be the biggest benefit of all. Yet, textbooks contain a number of problems too: they usually present surface-level understandings; their reading level is often too high for students; and they always contain unaddressed bias. Further, and perhaps most important, they do a bad job of presenting multiple perspectives about issues and events. Teachers, then, need to find resources on their own that can offer students more depth and more varied perspectives. These other types of resources exist. Libraries and museums will often loan entire boxes of varied materials to teachers. Nonprofits and NGOs sometimes provide materials about specific topics. And the Internet, of course, is awash in historical information. The challenge for teachers is creating the time to acquire these resources and learning how to use them, especially when teachers are so often overwhelmed by the other responsibilities of their jobs.

Even with all of these challenges, quality teaching in Social Studies is crucial. Social Studies helps to create a public that is literate about social and historical issues, can analyze problems through context, and has a global awareness of the challenges facing society. To create such a public, students must be presented with meaningful problems and asked to engage in analytical thinking. Forty-five minutes a week of Social Studies won't cut it, nor will a reductionist focus on test scores or teaching methods that keep students disengaged. Teachers face significant challenges in teaching Social Studies. But the urgency to confront those challenges in order to create this much needed public has never been greater.

9. Submit your essay, and then go relax – and feel confident about the quality of your work.

ARTICLES CITED

This is a list of articles cited in this book:

Berliner, D. C. (2005). The near impossibility of testing for teacher quality. *Journal of Teacher Education, 56*(3), 205-213.

Cochran-Smith, M. (2005). Teacher education and the outcomes trap. *Journal of Teacher Education, 56*(5), 411-417.

Schneider, J. (2012). Socrates and the madness of method. *Phi Delta Kappan, 94*(1), 26-29.

Vogler, K. E. (2005). Impact of a high school graduation examination on social studies teachers' instructional practices. *Journal of Social Studies Research, 29*(2), 19-33.

Vogler, K. E., & Virtue, D. (2007). "Just the facts, ma'am": Teaching social studies in the era of standards and high-stakes testing. *The Social Studies, 98*(2), 54-8.

61040200R00071

Made in the USA
Columbia, SC
20 June 2019